Praise for the Book

Supreme read! You may not recognize these CEOs' names, but the lessons they share resonate loud and deep.

– **Ludovic Beaufils** | Vice President Product Marketing, Whirlpool

I have always believed it is always about people. This book tells you how and why.

– **Neville Isdell** | ex-Chairman & CEO, the Coca-Cola Company and ex-board member, General Motors

A great book to teach you, or remind you, of some of the most important ideas that form the foundation of business and life success.

– **John Spence** | one of the Top 100 business thought leaders in America

This book is a must read for anyone who is or wants to be a true leader. It's new, fresh and the stories are supreme. *Supreme Leadership* will change you and the people you surround yourself with if you read it and use the very practical examples. This book will show you how to go from great to supreme.

– **Robert Shemin** | *New York Times* bestselling author

* * *

After you read *Supreme Leadership*, you will have gained sage wisdom that otherwise would have taken years to gather. Your leadership skills and confidence will skyrocket. I recommend this book to leaders of all types who want to make a difference for others while lighting the way.

Dr. John Spencer Ellis | CEO, National Exercise and Sports Trainers Association

This is the definitive leadership playbook. Follow the advice inside here and you'll learn what it takes be a leader worth following.

– **Paul Sohn** | bestselling author of *Quarter-Life Calling*, leadership coach and speaker

A powerful, practical guide that shows you how to make it to your company's 25th anniversary… from people who've done that and more.

– **David Burkus** | associate professor of leadership and innovation, Oral Roberts University; author of *Under New Management*

Nothing beats experience, especially in leadership. If you want direct knowledge from leaders who have faced what you will, Alinka Rutkowska brings you unfiltered, honest accounts directly from leaders who have been there.

– **Joshua Spodek** | Author of *Leadership Step by Step*

Now more than ever, the world needs strong, authentic, caring and committed leaders. The wisdom in these pages from such leaders is highly valuable and well worth the read.

– **Christine Kloser** | Bestselling and award-winning author of *The Freedom Formula* and founder of the Transformational Author Experience

Leaders Press

Thanks for your business

Tony White

SUPREME LEADERSHIP

Gain 850 Years of Wisdom from Successful Business Leaders

Alinka Rutkowska

1. Leadership. 2. Business communication. I Rutkowska, Alinka. II. Title.

ISBN 978-1-943386-21-5 (pbk)
ISBN 978-1-943386-22-2 (ebook)
Library of Congress Control Number: 2017918269

To Dad, who taught me to mind my own business,

and to Mom, who always believed in me

CONTENTS

You

You are a leader. And a smart one at that. How do I know?

First clue: you picked up a book.

Second clue: you picked up a book entitled *Supreme Leadership.*

You already know that books can change lives.

The goal of this one is to make you a more effective leader.

How do you do that?

You read on.

When you do, you'll gain 850 years of wisdom from successful business leaders.

How is that possible?

Easy.

To be able to deliver more than half a millennium of leadership insights I interviewed 34 CEOs who are celebrating their company's 25th anniversary the year of this book's publication.

34 times 25 equals... 850.

After the first 15 interviews, I noticed a trend. What allowed these leaders to succeed was their focus on one of these six leadership traits: passion, vision, adaptability, persistence, customer centeredness or relationships.

You will see yourself in these stories more than once. Within the pages of this book, you'll relive the mistakes these leaders have made and learn from them, so that you don't need to experience them yourself.

You'll discover the secrets to running a thriving 25-year company. You'll see laws of leadership that real people employed to achieve real results.

By the time you finish reading this book, you should be able to emulate featured leaders' strategies to lead your own company to its 25th anniversary.

But first, before you even get started, you need passion…

PART 1: PASSION

There is no greater thing you can do with your life and your work than follow your passions – in a way that serves the world and you.
-Richard Branson

One of the best-known entrepreneurs who swears that passion is the key to entrepreneurial success is Richard Branson. Although I would have loved to interview him for this book, this is, however, as we would say in Whirlpool (where I used to work), "out of scope." Sir Richard Branson started his mega-brand Virgin in 1970 when he was just 20 years old. After almost 50 years in entrepreneurship, his advice to budding entrepreneurs is to give their businesses a purpose and try to make a positive difference. Like most of the CEOs I feature, Branson maintains a people-conscious business model. By concentrating on purpose and difference, he maintains that a business that helps others will in turn give customers a reason to buy and other businesses a reason to work together.

Branson recommends maintaining control over your business by securing funding through ways that do not give away equity. He recommends using crowdfunding or even traditional bank loans to raise needed capital. Having to perform for investor satisfaction will likely lead to problems down the line, he claims. Branson advises retaining full ownership so business owners can avoid later problems. He said if he were to start all over today, this is the route he would take.

Branson is well known for espousing the importance of passion in business, as well as advising that launching a business simply to make money can easily result in failure. When launching Virgin Money in 1995, he admits to not feeling passionate about the idea of banking, so he instead chose to focus on his penchant for good customer service. He channeled his passion into making banking accessible and understandable for people, rather than focusing on the banking aspect. For Branson and his crew, taking risks ignites their passions. Creating the world's first commercial spaceline, Virgin Galactic, is surely not without risks. To that Branson said, "Our commitment to taking risks excites and enthuses our staff, as well as our customers. We've seen many brands stagnate in recent years. By innovating in the sectors where we are currently operating and taking the risk of entering new markets, we think Virgin can avoid the same fate."

Over the course of the interviews I conducted it became clear that successful leaders need passion to win big and celebrate 25 years in business. Let's take a closer look.

Tony White, enChoice

If you don't start with passion, you're probably not going to make it.

With offices across the United States and Europe, enChoice, Inc. is a multi-award-winning enterprise content management solutions company. Founded in 1993, this company helps customers improve business processes and protect critical information through software solutions and support to accelerate business efficiencies and competitiveness. When I asked Tony White, CEO of enChoice, to what he attributes his outstanding success, he said that without a doubt a business leader needs to have something to believe in and feel passionate about.

"If you don't start with that strong belief that you have something that is needed and you're willing to go the extra mile to make it happen, you probably will not be successful on your own." 25 years ago, Tony advocated the idea to go paperless. He felt the world was being flooded with paper and that it was time to solve what he saw as a huge problem by cutting down on the mounds of unnecessary paperwork.

Consider that in 1993 only 22 percent of American homes had a computer and that by 1997 home Internet availability would only be a mere 18 percent! So many things have changed since then and our concepts have broadened to shift much of our communications to electronic. In 1993, Tony's idea was a novel concept.

Once you have something you believe in and are passionate about, Tony's second recommendation for success is to turn that idea into something practical that the market will accept. "If you can show a customer a few elements of what is a more effective and efficient way of operating, they will say it sounds good, and they will buy it," he said. A paper-based insurance claims process used to take 10 days. When, however, Tony's company made the process electronic, the time was reduced to a mere half a day. Noting that successful companies are constantly trying to change to become more competitive, Tony recognized that if he offered them something that they could do early and become the pioneers — the early adapters — some were willing to do it.

Tony was careful to note that it wasn't always easy. "Making people change, as many know, can be very, very difficult. We generally all like to do things in the way we know best and the way we understand and feel the most comfortable. Part of the challenge in any type of ground-breaking endeavor is to convince people it's worth making that change, to grow out of their comfort zone. That's what you have to be able to do after having a belief and an idea." Tony admitted that although many ideas are great, some don't turn out well, and a big reason could be that the timing is wrong. "You have to have the right technology and the right market in order to launch a new idea. Often, change is too early," he said. For example, Tony noted that before the iPhone there were many attempts to create a small portable device that could do some of the things that the phone does today, but the timing was wrong and the technology wasn't yet ready.

I asked Tony if convincing people to change was one of the bigger obstacles his company had to overcome in the last 25 years.

He said the biggest obstacle he encountered was to come up with an economic model that worked for both the customer and his company's bottom line. When planning the business, he had to figure out how to show his customers that from both their point of view and his this was an economic way to go about doing business. The cost of doing what enChoice offers had ultimately to be profitable for them because otherwise they wouldn't have been able to survive for 25 years. "The internal economic model is the next most difficult thing after convincing customers to change because if you don't have that, you don't have a business to feel passionate about. Now, you can start off losing some money as you're trying to enter the market — and it's almost impossible not to — but you have to have a very clear plan as to when you will be able to make money. Otherwise, you'll have to sell your concept to somebody else, which is one of the reasons we are not a huge company. We have been very careful to maintain control over our own destiny. We never run out of money because we have an economic model that works."

I was curious to know whether Tony immediately figured out the model that worked for enChoice or had gone through several different attempts before finding something that worked.

He realized early on that they had to create recurring revenue by retaining customers in order to do multiple business with them. "A company will always have adjustments, because what you think will work is not exactly what you end up with. The most important thing we realized was that we had to create long-term customers who would either do business with us multiple times or who would pay us for a support contract. By having annual contracts, we were able to collect in advance for a year of service."

This recurring revenue was so crucial that Tony said without it, they could not have built their business. Otherwise they would have perhaps had to secure a venture capitalist. In Tony's opinion, they would have then ended up being under someone else's control. This wasn't something Tony wanted to do. While, admittedly, that path works for others, Tony believed that his company should control their own destiny. Echoing Richard Branson's advice, Tony said they didn't want to go out to the market and raise money. Instead they took loans from friends, family and management and a bank to raise initial capital. They built a model around a recurring revenue stream. Today about 40 something percent of their revenue is recurring, and that keeps them very nicely in business.

Creating the recurring revenue support model was the key to Tony's business success. Rather than getting a new customer, giving them a new business process by getting rid of their paper and then going away, they would propose to their customers that now that his company had solved their paper problem, they needed to stick around to support the new system. By charging 20 percent of the value of that cost system, they were paid annually every year. They ended up making more money from that than they did from the initial project. An additional cumulative bonus is that the more customers they got, the more revenue they earned.

The other benefit was that in the process of streamlining the customer's communications, they became what they call a "trusted advisor" for the customer. "In other words, if the customer's happy with what you're doing, they will not look for somebody else. They'll work with us because we already delivered for them. Most customers consider that to be more important than shaving a couple of dollars off the cost."

Tony feels that becoming a trusted advisor who provides quality and service is more important to a customer than price. Of course, you have to be competitive in your price, but if you can become the trusted advisor for your customer, the best customers are truly repeat customers. They know you don't have the customer acquisition cost to nearly the same extent. New customers want to know who you are and what you are offering, and will also look at alternatives. You win some of them and you lose some of them. Once a customer knows you — not always, but most of the time — they will tend to feel they have something that works already and it's a good deal for them. So why would they bother to look at other options?

Aside from the importance of recurring revenue, I asked Tony about what other laws of leadership he developed in the last 25 years that affected his business.

He explained that after becoming a customer's trusted advisor, the quality of your people is the next most important thing. "You have to have a very strong team. The members of your team are critical in order to get good people who can become trusted advisors to your customers. I couldn't possibly do all that on my own. We have more than a thousand customers, so obviously, we have to have good people; people who can go in and do that job and be respected and trusted by the customers."

Tony recognized that in order to hire and retain good people, he had to treat his people as his biggest asset after his customers. He treats his people well, by sharing his vision and passion with them and allowing them to feel like they're a big part of it. "That's why I always use the term 'team members'. We are not allowed to use the term 'employee' in our company because that implies someone just works for you and it's all about how much salary you pay them every month," Tony said. "We create this idea that we are all part of our team, that we approach projects together, and everyone is equally important. We try — and I believe we've succeeded — in keeping a very low rate of team member turnover."

EnChoice's turnover rate is far lower than typical companies. Tony admits that sometimes they lose people when they are offered a position elsewhere, but it doesn't happen often. "Retaining team members is key to our company's success. Over 25 years, we've built a solid team with a working model that is very difficult to compete with. Our combined experience in the industry is hundreds of people years with roughly 120 team members with an average experience level of 10 years in the business. Many veterans remain on the staff, having been with the company from the early beginning."

I was intrigued by how Tony was able to retain so many of his team members. Had he done anything in particular?

"To keep a high rate of team members we make sure to do the most important things," Tony said. "After one year of employment, team members get a stock option in the company. When everybody has some ownership in the company, it's very important because it makes them think about the little things, like turning off the lights at night to save money." EnChoice also offers other top benefits, including medical insurance and a 401(k). Since they compete with the best blue-chip companies, their team members have better benefits than even major companies like IBM. Although Tony recognizes that there are companies, such as Google and Netflix, where employees can take as much vacation as they want, they haven't gone to that level. Their benefits, however, are certainly better than their counterparts and even blue-chip companies.

EnChoice doesn't have a manufacturing plant. Tony feels

that his manufacturing assets are his people's intellect, so it's important to have good people. "I pay our people well," Tony said. By striving to pay 15 percent above the average rate for the job, he feels he gets 200 percent productivity in return from the team member. "In software, a good person can be ten times better than a weaker person. We look for the good people and then we pay them more and we look for even more from a contribution point of view from them. I think it's a big mistake to try to save money on people because in any business your people are your talent."

I know that leaders tend to read a lot, so I asked Tony which book has influenced him the most in the way he conducts business. His answer surprised me.

"I suppose as a young man many years ago, the book that influenced me the most was Ayn Rand's *Atlas Shrugged*. The book's message is based upon the author's philosophical system of Objectivism, with a primary tenet being that the moral purpose of life is to pursue your own happiness, or the concept of rational self-interest. You're responsible for your own future through your own performance. I've always believed that very strongly," Tony said.

Admittedly, he reads a lot and Tony counts many business books on his list, including Geoffrey Moore's *Crossing the Chasm,* which focuses on marketing high-tech products during the start-up period. As a business owner, Tony feels it's important to read a lot of history. "I've just read a book about Winston Churchill in South Africa, which is my original home country, and what he achieved and how he did it. I find that history can be a good indication of the future as well as the past. If we could learn more from history, we wouldn't make so many mistakes in the present."

As a last note Tony adds, "Another theory I gained from my business reading is that company values are more important than a business plan. We have very strong values at enChoice that we strive to stick to. One last value I'd like to mention is to strive for continuous improvement. In this world today, you have to be willing to be constantly changing. That's a value that we have: never stay the same. Keep changing."

While Tony directs the curious to check out his company by visiting his website, he is sure to point out that they don't tend to be egotistical. In keeping with their consistent and low-key style of management, he explains that even on their website they don't hype up their people but just talk about the company. By visiting www.enchoice.com, you can learn more about their values and what they do.

Eric Wenning, Wenning Entertainment

It really comes down to passion.

In 1993, Wenning Entertainment started out as Wenning's DJ Service where they performed at small events, parties and local weddings. The company has grown into a nationwide full-entertainment company. In addition to taking care of the music, they also offer event coordination, photography, cinematography, lighting and much more. Their growing company has now launched new divisions of the Wenning Family: Wenning Branding and Wenning Promotional.

Considering their diverse offerings, I wanted to know the No. 1 factor that Eric attributes their incredible success to and how it has affected the way he conducts business.

"It comes down to passion and drive and faith in God that he will bring me the right clients and the right connections. Passion means waking up and knowing you want to be successful as you pursue opportunities rather than run that daily rat race. Some days are more frustrating than others. You're going to have roadblocks and different hurdles that you need to overcome that day or within that time frame,"

Eric said. "But it's good to wake up and realize that I've come into something that I built and that I started from scratch. I didn't get this business from my parents. My dad wanted me to stick with a 9-5 job. He didn't want me to do an entrepreneur kind of thing. He wanted me to have safety and security. But nowadays there is no job safety; there is no job security. I took a risk and it's paying off. Now I have to keep on hustling with it."

The passion absolutely has to be there to keep an entrepreneur moving. I asked Eric what else he attributes his success to. I liked his play on words.

"You have to find good accountants. I don't mean accountants who take care of your money. I mean other people who are successful and hold you accountable. That's why we call them accountants," he said. "I have other friends in the industry who have been doing it as long as me, if not longer. We all hold each other accountable. Sometimes in business you get bogged down and you get worn out. But when you have other people acting as accountants, they build you back up and remind you why you got into this business and into this life. They remind you that you can't just give up. You can't have a negative attitude. You have to look at the positive outcomes and how far you've come."

I wondered what in the past 25 years was the biggest obstacle Eric's company had to overcome. His answer was surprising.

"Our biggest obstacle was very fast growth! Growing too big, too fast. We bit off more than we could chew, as they say, because we always said 'Yes' to our clients," Eric explained. "Instead of saying 'No', we would say 'Yes' and then find a way to make it happen. Whenever we had to do bigger shows — like live sound productions for a national touring artist — we had to find the right crew to handle that, and manage it properly, and then everything else as well."

I wondered how Eric's team managed to handle that growth. Did they increase their team or just work longer?

"All of the above. You're always going to be working longer hours when you're trying to expand or do something different. You have to find other crew who are more efficient and more knowledgeable in that area than you are, because whenever you're expanding, you might not be 100 percent knowledgeable. Take coding a website, for example. We find ways to do it and the people to do it. It works out well and they work out in becoming an asset to the company instead of a liability. Find the right people to help move you forward rather than just trying to learn everything yourself. You can't learn everything. You can't educate yourself on every aspect of every single technology out there. It's finding the right people that can do it for you and save time, because time is a big thing," Eric said.

I asked if Eric had developed any leadership laws that have impacted his business.

"Try to keep a cool head," Eric said. "In the entertainment world, things move very fast. A lot of people try to screw you to get ahead. It's a reality of show business — not show friends — so you have to keep that in the back of your mind. There are other people with other mindsets such as, 'I'm going to step on you to get another two steps ahead.' You always have to have a guard up, and keep yourself cool."

I wanted to know if Eric had developed company values that hang on the wall in the lobby or if his laws are more of an intangible thing.

"Definitely intangible. You can go on Amazon and buy motivational posters all day long, but it's really all about having a good relationship with your team and your staff. You have to be able to motivate them, move them forward, and be able to help them. That motivates them to work for the greater good rather than just getting through a 9-5 work day," he said.

I wondered about the level of turnover in Eric's type of entertainment business. Had he been able to carry many of his employees from the beginning of the company? I wondered if his business attracted people who would eventually leave to find other opportunities to pursue.

Eric confirmed what I suspected. "You're always going to have turnover in this industry. My assistant has probably been the longest running for about five years now. A lot of the DJs move on. They're with me maybe four or five years, seven years tops. My DJs start with me when they're in high school and work with me throughout college. It's a great part-time job because they work one, two or three days a week, but make more money than their peers make in a month. My guys have been set up for success part-time. I have trained them and taught them about business, work ethics and how to keep that drive alive. While I'm sad to see them go, it's always cool to see them go do something else they love and have a passion for; to go out and make themselves a success," he said.

I asked Eric if he was able to see 25 years ago that he would be able to take his company to where it is now.

"If you don't envision it, it's not going to happen. You have to be able to visualize your success and visualize what you want rather than simply saying you want to be successful. What does that success actually look like? Is it having a nice house, car, wife? Having a nice office? You have to visualize that success, because it won't just happen if you don't have a vision for it," Eric explained. "I set a goal for myself to be semi-retired by the time I turn 40. I'm not there yet, I still have a little bit to go. From where I'm at now, it's cool to look back and say I envisioned this and I envisioned that."

Does Eric use a particular method to visualize? Visualization is something that a lot of the motivational books talk about, and yet some people have a hard time actually doing it.

"I know some people put pictures of mansions and cars and yachts that they want by their mirrors. They look at that to drive them in the morning while they're getting ready for their day," Eric said. "I don't need any of that. I put my trust in God; that he's going to put me in the right places. I know what I want and I know what I want to achieve. I don't need to see a picture every single morning to give me motivation to go for it. Just being able to go into my own place of business and see all the happy customers is enough for me. That always keeps me going."

Since Eric is familiar with motivational books, I wonder which books have influenced him and the way he conducts business the most.

"Tony Robbins, Dave Ramsey and anything along those lines. I don't necessarily drink the Kool-Aid like others do. I educate myself by reading different educational and original entrepreneur books," Eric said. "I like to read about people who started a business from scratch, rather than reading about someone who made up ideas or stole someone else's ideas," Eric said. "I think about writing a book. Definitely, one day I will do that. The question is what kind of book and who would my target audience be if I wrote a book. I would include all my experiences in the entertainment world. Perhaps a self-help book for other DJs and entertainers."

To learn more about Eric and Wenning Entertainment, you can visit www.wenningent.com.

Wayne Reuvers, LiveTechnology

If you have a passionate team, then the entire company can be tenacious.

When you visit the website of LiveTechnology Holdings, Inc., the first thing you read is, "Unique Simplicity: saving businesses $641 million per year." If that doesn't make you curious, I don't know what will. This company has retained their position as the leader in omni-channel marketing and communications solutions for 14 years in a row. While they claim to have been "lucky enough" to evolve with the world's most successful brands, as they have taken on the challenge of an increasingly connected world, I doubt luck has anything to do with their incredible success.

When I asked Wayne what he attributes their success to, he said, "Beyond a doubt, it's tenacity. The difference between a smart person and an entrepreneur is that an entrepreneur never gives up. They're very tenacious. Even when the markets change, or the perception of the products, or whatever changes, they're prepared to segue; to go in different directions.

I've invested in a number of companies from early-stage companies to established companies and the one factor that has caused those companies that I've invested in to become successes was a tenacious leader. The factor has always been whether the leader was tenacious and was prepared to do whatever it takes to make things work. I was one of the original investors in a product called Panono, which was a camera that people threw in the air. These younger folks had the criteria and the success concept behind them, but they didn't have the tenacity to push it until the end. As soon as they started running out of money and hadn't hit their goals, they threw in the towel. The difference that makes businesses survive or not survive is tenacity," Wayne explained.

"Now, to make sure that tenacity is available, you need a lot of factors. Attitude is No.1. You need the best people. Skills are good, but not as vital. If you have a good team and those folks are passionate about what they do, and they're prepared to be very tenacious, then the entire company can be tenacious. That's the thing that in my view made Microsoft successful and what made people like Mark Zuckerberg successful. Every single time it was tenacity," Wayne said.

It's not just tenacity in surviving, but tenacity in thriving. "Zuckerberg had many, many options to leave early and sell his business at what were huge amounts of money. But he elected not to do that. And the same has happened to us. We've had offers from Microsoft, Google, Omnicom Group, and all were north of $100 million dollars at a time. Each time we've had the tenacity to walk away from what we thought was not the correct direction. Just because we were offered a lot of money didn't mean it was a good idea."

I wanted to know how Wayne is able to spot the tenacity he's seeking during the hiring process.

"There are some basic concepts we look for in potential employees. There's a concept called divergent thinking, a creative thinker who sees common problems from multiple different points of view. CEOs of successful companies are typically divergent thinkers who also surround themselves with divergent thinkers," Wayne explained. "A good example is a test where they give someone a paper clip and they say they have 10 minutes to come up with all the ways to use a paper clip. Divergent thinkers will typically come up with 120 to 150 different ways in 10 minutes. It sounds easy, but it's incredibly hard. Most of the world comes up with about 30 ways.

The interesting fact is that kids aged 5 to 7 will come up with over 100 ways to use a paper clip when they're kids, but as they go through the schooling system, they're actually taught to think more in line with everyone else. They're taught to stop thinking differently. Everything that they're taught in school is very much a structured concept. As they go through university, they're beaten down even more," Wayne said. "If you look at those kids who come up with great ways to think outside the box, by the time they leave university, they're taught to program in a certain style, they're taught to sell in a certain way. It's like the lemming syndrome: it's the same way everyone else does things. We look for folks who refuse to accept the status quo. We look for folks who are driven. If someone decides to be a nine-to-fiver, they can become a worker in a company, but they won't become a driver or a contributor of the growth of a company.

Some people are born organized, others have to figure out how to leverage tools to do so. I am one of these people who's incredibly disorganized, so I built tools to help me be organized. I realized right at the beginning that the key to success was organization," Wayne said. "When I was a one-person company doing contract work for one client, the first employee I hired was an administrator to help me do all the administrative stuff so I could focus on other areas of the business where I felt I was good. Organization is key," Wayne said.

When they bring new hires into the business, they look for understanding of the value and concepts of organization. "Anyone can be organized with the wonderful tools out there. But organization is based on two things. First, the weighting of information (in other words, of results) that you're going to achieve relative to the prioritization. Prioritization is driven from the weighting. In other words, anyone who's organized doesn't treat the 10 things they need to do as 10 things. They actually weight those 10 items based on the value they're going to contribute to the organization and to themselves. We look for divergent thinkers who are both enthusiastic and organized whether they are of the mentality that makes them naturally organized or whether they embrace tools that make them organized. The irony is most divergent thinkers aren't normally organized. But a clever divergent thinker is someone who embraces tools to help them," Wayne said.

I wondered about other interesting things that people might be faced with when wanting to become part of the LiveTechnology team.

"When I interview technologists, I look at their approach to things. I ask them questions that are driven more by logic and approach than specifically by technology," Wayne explained. "I use examples in everyday life to figure out the way they think. It's more important to me to figure out the way they think and figure out their attitude. Tom Watson, who was vice chairman of Omnicom Group, gave me some of the best advice I ever heard, which was, 'You should employ for attitude and train for skills. Don't employ for skills, because you can never train for attitude.' That was a really good wake-up call."

Wayne looked at what made companies like Microsoft and

Google successful. "I saw that in the beginning they employed people for attitude, but as they became bigger, they employed for skill. At the first level of recruitment, they looked at people with college degrees. But the very founders of Oracle, Google and Microsoft didn't have degrees. Not that they couldn't get degrees, but they made the decision that life was more important than continuing their studies. When they were small enough, they were very similar in their recruitment philosophy. But as they became big multinational companies, they ended up becoming like most multinational companies. The first filter of recruitment is based around people who have hit a bunch of benchmarks in the education system. From that point on, they focus on those people's achievements, successes and only finally, when they come for an interview, do they look at their attitude."

One of the reasons Omnicom has grown and has done very well is because they buy other companies, Wayne explained. "They own just over 900 businesses. Every time they buy a company, they're actually buying entrepreneurs, typically businesses of between 50 and 500 people. The other thing Omnicom founder Tom Watson said to me was, 'It's very easy to employ someone, but it's very hard to get rid of them.' From a psychological standpoint, as well as others. We as humans have a tendency to feel God-like when we employ. It makes us feel good to help someone. Tom advised me to make sure to get the correct people. Specifically, he said, 'Get the good people on the bus, but more importantly, get the bad people off the bus.' That really struck me. Having the chance to understand and learn from Tom Watson was hugely valuable for me as an entrepreneur," Wayne said.

The other thing they look for is a positive attitude. "Everyone says you can achieve anything with a positive attitude. I disagree with that. You need to have a positive attitude because that keeps you happy and committed, but you need a lot of other characteristics as well. The thing about a positive attitude is that it isn't as infectious as a negative attitude. Tom Watson also gave me another bit of great advice when he said, 'If you have a bowl of good apples and you put one rotten apple there, it turns all the good apples rotten. On the other hand, if you have a bowl of rotten apples and you add one good apple, it turns that good apple rotten.' He spoke about the water-cooler effect and why people always talk about the weather negatively rather than positively. It's the death of a company."

At LiveTechnology they make sure they don't have those negative elements, while taking pains to create a positive culture. "We have a squash center in our building. We have a full-time squash pro. We have yoga, Pilates, pool tables, a snooker table. Even though we're only 65 people, we have all of these facilities for them. We provide catered lunches. We realize that people who are physically fit and in good shape are also happy. Happy people don't move towards negativism that easily. If they're happy, they continue to be driven, committed, passionate and hopefully, the divergent thinkers we want them to be consistently. We give them freedom within constraints. We hold people accountable, making sure that they always know how well they're doing or how badly they're doing. But they need freedom to be able to make their own decisions within those constraints of accountability."

I am reminded of Whirlpool's European headquarters where I used to work. There was a swimming pool and a tennis court and a longer lunch break if people wanted to hang out at the pool and get an ice cream. People appreciated that a lot.

Wayne brought up a very interesting point. "Founders of these big companies start by hiring people with the required attitude. Probably these founders wouldn't even be employable in their own company if they were to apply now. When Microsoft made us the first offer a few years ago to purchase the company, they decided that 13 people were key executives that they wanted to lock in clauses for. I was obviously one of those people. The key business development person made an interesting statement to me. He said, 'Seven of your 13 people would not even qualify to have an interview at Microsoft.' I turned to him and asked, 'Doesn't that mean you're doing something wrong?' He explained that Microsoft had grown as a business that acquired other companies and that it was difficult to take those types of people and keep entrepreneurs interested in a big company. He said, 'Microsoft has grown everything — Office, Microsoft Word, Microsoft Excel, Microsoft SQL Server — from an acquisition from a company that was built by an entrepreneur'."

He told Wayne that the toughest part for Microsoft was that when buying companies, they had to make sure they could integrate them because they knew that the entrepreneur would leave. "It shed some light on why larger companies change their way of focusing from the attitudes first and skills last to turning that model on its head and actually focusing on skills and experience first and attitude last. It always gives smaller businesses like ours an opportunity to eat the crumbs from the giants' tables."

LiveTechnology's biggest obstacle during their quarter century in business has been their own success. "Every time we became successful, we became complacent. We've made mistakes. An investor bought five percent of our business for $12,500,000, which gave us this perceived value of $262,500,000 dollars, which we weren't worth at that stage. We had a tenth of the revenue we have now. But it made us think we were worth that. The minute you think something and your perception becomes reality, you make mistakes. It's a syndrome I like to call, 'Getting too big for your britches.' You think you're better than you are. Humility is a wonderful thing and if you can keep yourself humble, success comes with hard work, good attitude and clever thinking. And tenacity, of course.

Our biggest hurdle occurred when we thought we were too good, when big companies made us offers, invested in our business, or bought technology from us. For one of our clients, we solved their problem of sending out 1.3 billion emails a month of transactions and making sure these all had offers in them. It was a super success and made us a fortune in money, but we became complacent. Our biggest hurdle was success, because success drives complacency," Wayne said.

He is inspired by people like Elon Musk who have hit hurdles and were about to close down, and about to lose their business, but instead found a way around it. "If you read Peter Thiel's book *Zero to One,* you'll learn about when they had literally run out of money with maybe a week to go. We have also had cases where we got to the stage where we had been too successful and we relied on our success rather than what we did well. On three occasions, it almost killed us. Every time, we had to figure out what to do."

Rather than developing specific laws of leadership, Wayne says he has developed certain catchphrases and ways of being. "I always strive to be blunt. I find that people often don't say what they mean, but rather imply what they mean. A good example that I mention to every interviewee who comes in is, 'The word "try" is synonymous with failing.' They all look at me like I'm nuts. When someone succeeds, we say, 'Well done.' When they fail, we say, 'Well tried,' which is the nice way to say, 'You failed.' I believe in being blunt. I believe that we can only learn when we know the true facts. If things work, great. But if things don't work, you should never celebrate the effort that you put in. Instead, you should get some benefit from the failure. And the only benefit that you can get from failure is learning what not to do, or how to do things in a different way. I tell people not to celebrate failure, but to learn from failure. I don't believe in congratulating a person for putting in the effort."

Wayne said that everything comes down to results. "It's not about experience. It's about results. Whenever I bring people on board, I draw on the board to illustrate how people are paid by time when they work for companies. But companies are paid for delivery, unless you're like an Accenture or one of those companies paid for time. But in most cases, companies are paid for producing something. In our case, it's for producing output for large Fortune 100 brands. If it takes us three times as long to do something, we lose money. When you've got margins of 30 percent, if you increase the time it takes to do something by a third, you don't just wipe out your margin, you actually make a loss. Most people don't get that. Time is not equated to results. In other words, when we work for one of our clients, if we take longer, we don't get paid more. We actually lose more money," Wayne said.

"Everything needs to focus on the result. You have to start thinking about the result and work backwards. We call that, 'Begin with the end in mind.'" Wayne explained. "When you work backwards, it's easier when you figure out the milestones or the goals you will need to get there. One of the first things I tell people that join LiveTechnology is to get a pile of Post-it notes and establish their own five-year goal, because most people in this world just have these variable gray goals. You can't say, 'I want to be living this way,' or 'I want to own a house.' If you don't tie a specific date and time to something, you will never accomplish your goal.

I always tell people to write down the goal. If it's a five-year goal to be married and have kids or to live in a five-bedroom house or own a yacht, they need to write it on a piece of paper and put it on their mirror and then they need to look at five steps to that," Wayne said. "So if it's a five-year goal, they need to look at the four years in between and actually write what they are doing to work toward their goal. And they start backwards. Every morning when they get up, they need to look at this year's goal, which is driving towards the end goal at the end of five years. So when they're brushing their teeth or combing their hair in the morning, they see their goal next to the mirror. I believe if they have their goal in their mind, they will be successful," Wayne said. "All the people who work within LiveTechnology are all driven by a goal and by results. We use our own internal tools like LiveProject to show how far they are from their goal, or whether they've hit their milestone on the way to the goal. It all comes down to making sure people understand performance. As long as they understand that, humans are amazing. They can figure out how to be better. But if you don't give them numbers, they can never improve. So our leadership is very simple; we are results- driven and direct. None of this sort of implied concept."

Wayne places great emphasis on facilitating communication through visual means. "Everything has to be visual at LiveTechnology. We don't believe in email to communicate issues. We have tools that allow people to snapshot the systems and highlight and mark up and edit. We use that internally to help communication because the downfall of anything is bad communication. The reason people get divorced is because the husband and wife miscommunicate or misunderstand. The reason clients get upset with company suppliers is because of miscommunication. It can be around delivery, what was expected, what payment plans were, or miscommunication between employees and teams."

Wayne is a big reader, so naturally I wanted to know which books have influenced the way he conducts business.

"The single best book I've ever read is *Made in America* by Sam Walton. He was one of the most amazing people. Sam basically was a humble guy who wanted to build one store. Before you knew it, he'd built one of the largest retailers, one of the largest companies on the planet. He was a humble person. That's the book I recommend to anyone. As new employees come on at LiveTechnology, it's the first book we give them to read," Wayne said.

"Another phenomenal book I read was *The Master Switch: the rise and fall of information empires* by Tim Wu. It teaches how multitudes of independent entities form new networks that eventually become regulated and controlled. They talk about everything from radio networks, original newspaper networks that then became consolidated, cable television where farmers used barbed wire to transmit television that was bought out by the John Malones of the sport to form the cable empires, to the cellular empires. It's a very interesting thing because we're seeing the same happening online with Tencent, the big Chinese company buying other companies. Facebook buys companies. Microsoft buys companies. Google buys companies. *The Master Switch* was written a few years ago but it is absolutely phenomenal," Wayne said.

Another book Wayne loves is called *The Most Powerful Idea in the World: a story of steam, industry, and invention* by William Rosen. "What used to happen is ships would sail from Ireland to the U.S., take cotton back to Ireland, and then different goods back to the U.S. There was no schedule. This book illustrates how civilization is founded on the concept of time, and ultimately schedules," Wayne explained. "The minute these two guys scheduled when the ship would arrive and when it would leave, the farmers started scheduling when they would harvest. Then the transport companies, the wagons and trains started tying into those schedules. The ultimate result is the container that we all know now that accounts for almost all the shipping in the world, because the packaging became optimized based on scheduling. It's an amazing book that shows you how something like steam ended up having such a multitude of knock-on effects.

Another great book is *Diamonds, Gold and War* by Martin Meredith. I'm originally from South Africa and took my business from South Africa into the U.S. This is another interesting book that shows how some powerful people ended up taking control of different industries in the 1800s. It was the British, and people like Cecil John Rhodes, who weren't good people. They were actually terrible people. But in those days, it was easier for evil people to take control," Wayne said. "Nowadays, it's normally good people who take control. Mark Zuckerberg, who owns a fairly sizable portion of the world's communication, is actually a philanthropic person who does a lot of good stuff. The world has changed in that we have good people who are more powerful. That book is just fantastic in that it shows you how these people in the 1700s and 1800s ended up dominating these industries in similar ways to how it happens today in this information age and this information economy."

To learn more about Wayne and LiveTechnology you can find him on LinkedIn or visit www.livetechnology.com.

Mark Schena, Arrayit

If I were to distill our key to success to a single word, that word would be "passion".

When I asked Mark Schena, CSO (Chief Science Officer) of Arrayit Corporation — a leading life-sciences company providing innovative products and services to empower scientists and clinicians to explore genomes — to what he attributes his success, he replied, "If I were to distill it to a single word, that word would be 'passion'." Mark feels fortunate to wake up every day empowered by the fact that his company's products have the potential to improve lives, and in a longer-term sense, to make the world a better place. It's a personal thing for him, as he loves being a scientist and says the passion for doing innovative science in the great workplace they have has served them very well for over 25 years.

Wondering if developing passion had been a sudden thing for Mark, I asked how long he'd wanted to be a scientist.

"Starting in junior high school, I became pretty single-minded about becoming a scientist from that point on. I was lucky to have discovered early on not only what I wanted to do but also the ability to do it." Feeling passionate about becoming a biochemist, Mark went on to get his doctorate. He says he has a very fulfilling life, and enjoys the fact that he gets to wake up every day and discover new things. As a scientist, he is grateful for the ability to impact the world. The multitude of services Arrayit offers reads like a scientific journal with a long list of diagnostic applications, platforms, tests and high-tech products. "Obviously what we do is quite technical, but at the end of the day, a lot of the contributions are also practical. We're seeing that with our company, especially as we increasingly move into the healthcare space."

When I congratulated Mark on his 25-year anniversary in business, he said something surprising:

"It's difficult to be in business for 25 years."

That's kind of sobering, and yet a relief at the same time! While living the dream is fantastic, I was curious about the biggest obstacles Mark had to overcome in order to celebrate a quarter of a century in business. Tony from enChoice eschewed investors, preferring to borrow money from friends, family, management and banks, but when Mark faced the same decision he went in the other direction. "Probably our biggest obstacle has been access to high-quality growth capital," Mark said. "It's a financial consideration. We address the challenge by being very selective about our lenders and our investors. We try to run an efficient, profitable company to minimize our growth capital requirements." He addressed the financial challenges his company faced by making sure that they remained profitable. This had the built-in advantage of allowing them to operate with fairly modest growth capital requirements.

I asked Mark which laws of leadership he'd developed in his 25-year career and how they had specifically impacted his business.

Like Tony, Mark found that treating people well, both customers and employees, was a key component in their success. "Ultimately, business is all about the people. Our philosophy is that we endeavor to run a company based on very high standards. We try to put fundamental principles like honesty, integrity and loyalty at the very high end of the spectrum." Mark has seen over the last 25 years that if they do right by their employees, customers, B2B partners and investors, that tends to serve their company well. They've developed a personal rapport with their suppliers and customers, and that's been very important over the years.

When conducting my interviews, I noticed the trend that there was a certain loyalty factor that inevitably came into play. It seemed to be very common amongst the companies that have been around for 25 years to treat others well. When I shared my thoughts with Mark, he agreed.

Mark has obviously done more than a few things right. I was curious to know if he'd learned anything from books about how to conduct business. Although he admitted his answer may be partially self-serving, he said the book that most influenced his business was one he wrote. *"Microarray Analysis* was published some years ago by J. Wiley & Sons. It's a textbook on microarray technology, which is the fundamental science behind our company. The reason my book has been important is because we've found that by understanding both the theory and the practical underpinnings of the science that our company is built on, we were able to make better products, and to address new markets in a very efficient way. That's becoming particularly important as we move from the bench to the bedside."

Mark explained that like a lot of life sciences companies, while they started as a research company, they're moving increasingly in the direction of having an impact on the lives of patients in the healthcare systems. Whether it's research products or clinical products, understanding the science at a very deep level helps them make better products. "Even though I wrote it and it was a painful process to do so, it's probably the book that has impacted me the most. We find at Arrayit that we go back to the science on a regular basis to make sure that our products are really sound."

Mark has written a number of other books that have been equally important. His other books cover particular scientific methods and specialty concepts. *Microarray Analysis,* however, as a foundational piece, helps his company to keep the methodological principles in mind as they develop new products. Going to the very deepest level to ensure their products are as compliant and as easy to use as possible has given them an advantage in the marketplace.

Lastly, Mark mentioned that because Arrayit is a U.S. based company, they manufacture all of their products in the States, and sell them in the U.S. and abroad. "What we're doing is a small piece of invigorating American manufacturing. We make products here and export them to expand the prosperity of the country. We try to do our part every day."

Now that's passion!

To find out more about Arrayit, the curious can either visit www.arrayit.com or Mark's LinkedIn profile to drill down into some more professional detail.

What about you? Have YOU got passion? If you do, now you need to make sure you have... vision.

PART 2: VISION

I was just like a lot of show business personalities who work away quietly at their craft for years, and then, suddenly, they get the right break and make it big. I was an overnight success all right, but 30 years is a long, long night.
-Ray Kroc, McDonald's

John Maxwell in his bestselling book *Laws of Leadership* opens with the story of Mac and Dick McDonald, the two brothers who started what would eventually become the most successful fast food industry in history. Although the business sporting their name would grow to become a worldwide multi-billion-dollar corporation, it wouldn't happen under the McDonald brothers' leadership. Ray Kroc, a 52-year-old milkshake machine salesman suffering from diabetes and arthritis, had the vision to see potential and took immediate action.

When Kroc learned that the McDonald brothers were using eight of his milkshake machines at their California restaurant, he was curious to check out their business. Upon arrival, he was stunned by the effectiveness of their simple operation. After several years of experimentation, Mac and Dick McDonald had figured out that hamburgers were their best sellers, and concentrated on being a very efficient, yet family-friendly burger restaurant. Their menu was simple. Their food was locally sourced. And their combination worked.

Kroc had the vision to take their recipe for success — food with consistently high quality combined with standard uniform methods of preparation — nationwide. Kroc became an agent for the brothers and within one year of his first visit, he opened the first franchise outside of Chicago. A mere four years later, he had opened 102 McDonald's restaurants!

The two McDonald brothers didn't envisage that the number of restaurants would eventually grow to tens of thousands of franchises all over the planet. In fact, they didn't even think their restaurants would survive in colder climates. But Ray Kroc knew they would. In 1961, he bought out the McDonald brothers for $2.7 million. Ray Kroc had a bigger vision, which was taking the operation wide through franchising, and in purchasing real estate in suburban areas in order to become the No.1 fast food chain in the world. "Getting involved in real estate was the beginning of real income for McDonald's," Kroc was known to have said.

The idea to consider a franchise from a real-estate point of view had to have been ground-breaking at the time. I was curious to see if the CEOs I interviewed shared Ray Kroc's "bigger" mindset. I wanted to know if they also had the ability to peer into the future.

Indeed they did.

Guy Akasaki, Commercial Roofing & Waterproofing Hawaii

Success comes down to casting vision.

When studying the successes of these CEOs, I never fail to be amazed by the variety of perspectives they share with me. Although many share common core values, each CEO is invariably unique and brings a distinctive history to the table. When I congratulated Guy Akasaki, of Commercial Roofing & Waterproofing Hawaii, Inc., on his company's 25th anniversary, I asked which No.1 factor he attributes his success to.

"When you look at the family of companies we have — or really any organization — success comes down to casting vision," Guy explained. Casting vision is the ability to communicate ideas and visions so that others make your vision their own. "It's one thing to have a vision or a mission statement that you see displayed on the wall in the lobby. But it's another thing to buy in; to live and operate by those core values of the organization. For us it's to work together as a team of professionals who combine our experiences and talents to be on the cutting edge of technology in our industry. And the most important part is to exceed the client's expectation."

Guy explained that sharing a core vision covers everything from the harmonious handling of crises and how employees get along with each other, to their systemic approaches and methods of operation. Everything fits within those core values. Talent can be learned: skill sets, mechanics, accounting and finance, Guy said. "But without having the blood running through the infrastructure that feeds the organism that is the company, it has no life. And at that point, it's perishable. Keeping that blood flowing is incredibly important to the life of the company."

Recently Guy spoke to a group of young entrepreneurs. While they were excited because they had vision and values, Guy noted that not uncommonly they didn't yet have strong values. He likened their phase in business life to when a young teenager gets his first car. Although he's never driven before, he's seen people driving and thinks he already knows how to do it. He holds those keys in his hands. He's on top of the world. He thinks nothing can go wrong and everything will go his way. But he doesn't yet realize the responsibility that's necessary behind driving, whereas adults already understand it because they have experience.

Guy told the young group, "One day you won't be able to tell what is right and what is wrong. You won't be able to tell your left hand from your right. One day, like surfing, you won't be able to tell what is up or what is down, because you're going to be tumbling in the water. You're going to be looking at a line that shows white on one side, and black on the other, and it's going to be so razor sharp and precise. But as you walk closer to that line, it will fuzz out. When you reach your forties, the line won't be as sharp or as pristine as it once was. As you draw closer, it will become pixelated. Eventually the white and black will become gray. And then suddenly you're in a mist."

Integrity, honesty, commitment and determination are some of the core values that are important to most CEOs I interviewed. "It's those core values combined with your own moral compass that determine not only who you are going to be, but where you're going to go. Just like the character in the movie *The Karate Kid*, you must be able to close your eyes and navigate the treacherous waters that you'll inevitably fall into when you're running a business. The intangible values are important in building an organization that can create a platform to give back to the community, as well as benefit from the community."

It sounds so easy, right? Figure out your core values and your business will flourish. I was curious to know if Guy always had the same moral compass and core values. Was he born with direction, or did it take him a while to figure things out?

"We are all born with direction, yet we are like horses, believing what society tells us to be. During training, horses wear blinders on their eyes so they learn only the one thing that they're taught. Why do they wear blinders on their eyes? So they cannot look at the horizon in a very broad perspective. They are forced to think and look only inside the box," he said.

Guy has made it a point to share with young people that they should not despise their small beginnings, but to look instead at the depth and width of the opportunities before them. He shared a story with me about the importance of knowing where you come from. When he was just starting out in business, he overheard his wife ask his mother if he had always been the way he was. His wife said that anything he touched he wanted to turn into a business. He figured out how much it would cost to start. What he could do to make money from it. He started to shape everything from a financial perspective. His wife complained to his mother that there might be something wrong with him. She wanted to know if he had been like that when he was a child?

At first his mom said, "No, I don't think there's anything that strange about Guy." And then she paused. "Wait a minute... I remember now. We were military, so we traveled a lot. I recall Guy would go to the military housing and he would collect all the little broken toys from the sandboxes and bring them home. He'd dirty up my kitchen floor, and I'd get really irritated because he would bring all these broken toys inside the house. He would take them apart, taking the pieces from the broken ones to add to others to make them whole. Then he would set up inside a military pup tent and display the toys that he fixed, selling them for one or two cents each."

But that wasn't all. His mother went on to say that during Halloween the year before, she had bought Guy and his brothers a toy called Creepy Crawlers. Guy explained that the toy had little insect molds where you put a plastic polymer inside, and after it cured, the polymer took on the shape of the insect. Guy and his brothers loved the polymer because it was luminescent. They'd make spiders and centipedes, and when they shined a light on them, the polymer insects would glow in the dark.

Guy's mother continued her story. "The following year during Halloween, Guy attached two pup tents together to form a long hallway and covered the top with thick blankets so that it was very dark inside. Then he and his brothers hung all of those luminescent and black insects they'd made on the inside of the tent. Guy made his brothers hide in the tent flaps while he went around the neighborhood and told all the kids that he had a haunted house. The kids would come and pay a penny to come to the haunted house. Because it was dark the kids couldn't see anything inside as they made their way through the tent. Guy's brothers would scream at them from the tent flaps and jump out to scare them. The kids would run out screaming to find Guy sitting at the other end of the tent on an army blanket."

Back then Guy said they only had comic books such as Ironman, Archie and Thor. He would sit outside the tent, waiting for the kids to come through to pay the one penny for going through the haunted house. While the kids waited for their friends to come through, they would sit down by Guy and start to read his comic books. Guy's mom told his wife, "You know what Guy did? He charged the kids a penny to read his comic books!"

As Guy recalled that long-ago scenario, he said how interesting it was to see that even back then there was a purpose and a design in his life. “You often fail to see that design as you move forward in your life because you have so many things that affect you in society. You wear blinders, trained to be what society wants you to be. Possibilities, hopes and aspirations are pretty much squelched because you look within the glass jar, rather than look from outside the glass jar. When you look at your life from the perspective of how you develop your core values, you will see how your values are personified well before you become who you will eventually become.”

I recall that when I was a child, I painted a little. To be honest, they were terrible pictures. I liked the creative part of it, but then I would set up a shop at home and sell them to my parents. I shared this story with Guy.

“See? The DNA was in you, too,” he laughed.

But success takes more than simply having the makeup, doesn't it? Guy went on to build an incredible family of companies with his skills. There are many people that we could call smart or creative, but then they don't do anything with their gifts. I'm curious to know why some make it and some don't. Surely every businessperson hits roadblocks along the way. Yet some don't give up. Could this be the difference? I asked Guy what has been the biggest obstacle for him. Has there been anything standing in his way during his years in business that made him feel that he might not be able to make it to 25 years?

"There's actually been quite a few of those times," Guy said. "A lot of them were due to economic cycles and unforeseen circumstances. I learned to look at cycles and I will get into that a little more. I've been through about two cycles so far, and now I see the third cycle coming forward. A lot of the leveraging in our companies is for the purpose of being able to leverage what we know through experience is coming. While nobody can really anticipate, we know it will be full of cyclical upturns and downturns. You can't wear blinders in business. You have to keep your eye on the horizon at a different level. You can't think that things will continue to go along in a perfect manner."

Hold onto your hat, because Guy's ability to leverage is more than phenomenal. He explained that for construction and the economy at large, they created Commercial Roofing, their founding company for the past 25 years. Hawaii is a signatory state, so for the union side they started another company called Honolulu Roofing. Under this company, they do a lot of new projects with the union. Additionally, they have Allied Pacific Builders, a general contracting company. They do renovations for the military and the federal government. They have Allied Pacific Builders Guam, which they started on Guam because of the military buildup that was occurring there.

For the energy sector, they started GreenPath Technologies, which is a renewable energy company. They're very familiar with photovoltaic assembly, applied photovoltaics and building integrative photovoltaics. In that company they also do research and development. Another company they own buys kilowatt hours that they engineer, or EPC, engineering procurement construction. They install solar photovoltaic arrays onto nonprofits for free, getting tax credits and subsidies in return. They generate revenue streams for 20-25 years with escalating increases every year, like an annuity.

Guy's commercial brokerage company handles the assets for one of the largest unions in the state of Hawaii. They do property management leasing and commercial and industrial real-estate investment.

I suddenly understood why Guy's wife asked his mother all those years ago why he wanted to start a business from everything he touched!

"We take all these different companies and integrate them. You're probably thinking, 'What?' Roofing, construction, research and development to renewable energy, commercial brokerage — how does it all connect? It seems so discombobulated. But I think in 25 years, I've come to understand the obstacles that I had to face. And to do that I had to look at the economic cycles. Like when administration and government changes, the landscape changes as well," Guy said.

He noticed in Hawaii, and in the mainland as well, that there was usually an economic cycle of about 10-15 years which generally tended to follow the real-estate cycle. "When you look at the real-estate cycle from the high point of one cycle to the next high point, it resembles a bell curve. It goes up, comes down, and goes up again. And if you look over a 30-year period, you'll notice that the means will always rise." Even though we feel the gap between the bell curve, the drop from high point to high point tends to be about 10-15 years. To get through two cycles will take 20-30 years. "With that rise, you follow the economy, and it generally trends first in the real estate. The luxury housing generates a lot of activity. Right after that, a lot of commercial infrastructure starts to come in: malls, shopping centers and stores. Then the next thing that comes into play is urban housing and suburban housing. Then while that's happening, in comes commercial infrastructure on the outer limits of the non-density areas of population. After that in this cycle, you start to see a build out of industrial properties to be able to support the next wave. Banking starts to loosen up. Boutique shops pop up. You see restaurants galore. You see consumer confidence — which is an indicator that drives any economy to ascend to a very high point. It's usually around that apex of the 10-15-year mark. We're about maybe 90-95 percent of getting there at this point. And then something usually happens, whether it be something catastrophic, or a policy, or an issue, then comes a correction in the market. You have to be ready to anticipate that," Guy said.

Guy asked if I'd ever heard the phrase, "wine, women and song". "During those 10-15-year high points, many feel confident that the good times will never end. They feel sure that tomorrow will be even better than today. In the Old Testament, Joseph said that in times of famine, you should plan and then execute on the next cycle, which will be a season of feast. With that simple precept, Pharaoh gave Joseph the responsibility to do so, and Joseph exploded the assets that Pharaoh had. In the times that it was fat, he put money, product and grain aside for the times it would be tough, rather than enjoying wine, women and song.

During the famines, Joseph took those same assets that he built in the reserves during the time of feast, and gave back to the community. He started to do contrary to what people would ordinarily do, which would basically be to hunker down, and just hole in for that time. With his reserves he was able to reach out to neighboring countries, to the Pharaoh's kingdom and to all the people. As a result of his careful planning and execution, they became even stronger, because Pharaoh had the resources to expand in a time when other countries could not," Guy said.

What a history lesson! By learning to play the long game, and understanding long-term cycles, Guy was able to ride out each cycle and plan and act accordingly. I was curious to know whether in 25 years of business, Guy had consciously developed or had written down any of his personal leadership laws.

"Listen more, rather than listen to answer back. A lot of times people listen with the intention to give an answer back, or to talk back rather than listen with the truest of intentions of actually hearing," he replied.

A business person may think that success is a destination, but success is more of a process than a destination. "Whereas people might see today that you've had success, it's important to remember that success is a process; a very interesting journey. Remember the cycles? If you get the feeling you've 'arrived', it's really the day that you've got to start going in the opposite direction, which is down. The day that people say you've succeeded — and that day that you earnestly understand that you've come a long way — is really where you are at your most vulnerable. It's critical that that same passion and vision that you had when you first started continues to remain alive as you continue to strive towards that next point.

"I wouldn't say it's a law, but as an entrepreneur you need to be able to cast vision to your team," Guy said. "Along those same lines you also need to know that betrayal can and does come from the closest of your circles. You will see that as the members of your circle begin to role-play the values that you embrace. Sometimes the obstacles that you have to face are in the closest of your circles. It can have a debilitating effect on what you do. Part of it is what they call the 'crab mentality' — or the idea that in a bucket of crabs there are those who will pull down those trying to escape. It's an 'if I can't have it then neither can you' mentality. Sometimes it is in those closest circles where you would think absolutely nothing would happen where it happens. And so your faith in mankind wanes."

Another one of Guy's teaching moments comes from the movie *Lethal Weapon,* with Mel Gibson and Danny Glover. "There's one insight between him and his partner. They're talking about working with each other. Mel Gibson is a crazy policeman while Danny Glover is the smart, predictable, strategic policeman. So after they have a few drinks, Mel goes, 'Man, you should've seen what happened to me. Look. Right here. I got shot by a 45-caliber bullet.' He lifts up his shirt and says, 'See this mark right here? That was a 45-caliber bullet.' Glover says, 'Well, look at my leg. I got stabbed by a knife.' And Mel says, 'I got stabbed by three knives. Look at my back.' And they start to share all of their wounds."

Guy said it's the same thing in business, recognizing the struggle to remain able to embrace values, instill vision, and give opportunity to others, while being afraid of betrayal. "You must know that as you begin to grow, betrayal will occur in your closest circles and you cannot allow that to cause you to think less of any people that you work with. Or even within the circle that is close to you. It veils or it causes you to hold back. It causes you to insulate yourself, and when you begin to do that, that's really the beginning of the fall. Unfortunately, that's a facet of human interpersonal relationships that is a part of life. All of this has to be built into the values that you believe, because at the end of the day, if you don't anticipate these things, you're going to become a very old cynical person — about people, about life at large, and more so about you as an individual."

While the mechanical tools of accounting and other things in business are important, Guy emphasized that intangible values transcend beyond the expectations in the good times. "That set of values — the core values of who you are, what you are, what you believe in — is the one thing that will take you through. For young people who start businesses, their initial dream is to make a lot of money. Their only dream is that they've only had opportunity that works. The real test is when things don't work. The elements and components of seeing through life is still the same."

Guy is not a voracious reader, but he claims to draw from a lot of book resources. "There's a lot of financial books, but none specifically. Zig Ziglar. Maxwell. Covey. Books about financial marketing. I look at principles. You've heard about the 20/80 rule, that 20 percent of the people do 80 percent of the work? I tend to look at a lot of things that have to do with trends and statistics. I love the books that have to do with quantum sciences. I love books that make me think that the impossible is possible because that broadens my perspective. I enjoy different books that make you think outside the box. There's no one specific resource that I see myself drawn to reading."

Guy recounted a humorous story when I asked how readers can find out more about him. "The best thing to do if you want to find me is to Google my name. Before I really started getting into the Internet stuff — years and years ago — I was asked to join a board of contractors that reach from the east coast to the west coast, servicing all of the Fortune 500 companies. This was at the last general Roofing Contractor Association, the oldest and largest association in the United States. I said, 'Sure. I can put together a profile on what my company has done, what we can provide, and what we can commit to the organization.' They replied, 'Oh, that's not necessary. We already know everything we need to know about you.' I thought this was getting a little weird, so I asked, 'Who have you been talking to?' And they were laughing, because they were far ahead of the curve at that time. They asked me, 'Guy, ever heard of Google?'"

Donald Pell, Donald Pell Gardens

It's about finding people that you're excited to work with who believe in your vision and want to make that their own.

While some CEOs know from a young age what their driving ambition will be, I was curious to meet others who successfully managed to build a solid business from what might look like happenstance. Could vision be developed? Donald Pell offers landscape design and consultation, garden maintenance and management, agronomy, arboriculture, permaculture, masonry and carpentry. I wondered if he'd always known that he wanted to be in the landscaping business.

"No, I didn't. I was working on trying to be a professional musician out of school, and I didn't go to college because I immediately started working on recording projects. My family had a little nursery, and I'd started doing some small garden jobs as a way to feed myself, when I met a designer who thought I had a good eye. I wasn't even sure what she meant!" The designer encouraged Donald to educate himself through the industry, and that was the start of a new career 25 years ago. "I feel extremely fortunate that landscaping design found me; I became so obsessed with it. I was in love with the opportunity to be an asset to our community. That's how I look at what we do. I think that is very powerful as well; we look at what is our role in the community."

While Donald's initial career beginnings may have been circumstantial, once he set out to develop his landscaping design firm, he was all in. Donald is confident that the No.1 factor in his company's success was having a succinct vision. Like Guy, Donald feels passionate about casting vision; communicating to their staff and the general public what it is they provide, and finding people who are excited to work in the landscaping field, and who have the ability to deliver exceptional services. He has recognized the importance of having the right team members and clientele. "I think in the end it's about finding people that you're excited to work with who believe in your vision and want to make that their own, and not really having an ego about control, but trusting your instincts, and then checking the data to see that you're progressing as a team in the right direction."

Donald advises small businesses to start building datasets, even something simple like a P&L to understand how to go about monitoring progress so you have a good handle on the details. "So many entrepreneurs build because that's what is innate in them. They want to get out and do for themselves, and they don't all necessarily have the background to be able to understand all the finances or how to track data in terms of progress. I think that's been a very powerful tool for us to trust our instincts, but then to follow those up with hard data, and make sure we're progressing in a healthy way. That has been a huge asset in us having the success we've had."

Donald's vision continues to grow as his business thrives. "We'd love to do much more institutional work and be able to touch more people in that regard and change the way people think about space. There's this idea of democratizing space to create very healthy places for people to live in. That's a very exciting idea to me that I look forward to expanding upon."

He acknowledged a pretty common issue many new business owners face which is not saying no often enough, especially in the beginning when trying to build your business and acquire new clients. He recommended focusing on interviewing the client as opposed to having them interview you. "There's been a lot of power in that for us. This definitely helps you fully understand from your perspective if you can really help a client, or if you even want to take them on."

Next, Donald shared the laws of leadership he developed during his 25-year career that he felt has impacted his business. "I'd say the entire focus really has been on an outcome of excellence for every project we work on, focusing on that and that alone. We look to develop something that is world-class, and provide exceptional client services, and focus on what we've done well, and then later to analyze acutely what we could have done better. Our whole team is so excited by the fact that we're looking to be a world-class design firm, and not just a local company. We're always searching for something better, always thinking about the project right up until it's been completely executed."

Aside from the outcome of excellence and introspection, Donald recommends having a team who gets excited about providing something that's exceptional: a team who is receptive to the cast vision. Donald credits Jim Collins and his book *Good to Great* with helping him develop a solid management style. "Collins helps you focus on your core competency and finding the best people for the jobs. He recommends against trying to pigeonhole people because they came into your company doing one job. I'm always asking people where they want to go, and that's whether that's in our organization or some place else. If it's some place else, we work hard to try to help them get there," Donald said. "I think we've had great successes. Even ex-employees send us fantastic jobs. But at the core it's clearly understanding what we do very well and just sticking to that, and educating the entire team on that, and having a succinct brand and marketing program about just those things."

Donald's love for his craft is apparent in his philosophy, which embraces the idea that "building gardens is about creating a powerful experience of place and time" and in helping nature meet man's architecture by creating a harmonious whole. To learn more about Donald Pell and read about his philosophy, you are invited to visit www.donaldpell.com.

Shanin Specter, Kline and Specter

Always promote values such as preparation, hard work, integrity, loyalty, kindness, responsiveness, attention to detail, flexibility, and a strong interest in continual improvement.

"We concentrate our law practice in the representation of persons who are catastrophically injured. Those cases arise out of medical malpractice, or a defective product, or a serious motor vehicle accident, or improperly maintained premises, or some other type of circumstance where there has been fault that has led to a very serious injury," Shanin explained to me during our interview. His victories combine monetary awards for their clients with notable news-making remedies, and the corporation's success is undeniable: he has obtained more than 200 jury verdicts and settlements in excess of $1 million, and more than 50 case resolutions — including 16 verdicts — greater than $10 million.

Among Shanin's verdicts are a whopping $153 million against a major automaker, and $109 million against an electric power company. His legal victories have included industry-changing cases involving medical malpractice, defective products, medical devices, premises liability, motor vehicle accidents and general negligence. "The firm is the largest personal injury firm in Pennsylvania, and it's one of the largest in the United States," Shanin said. "I would attribute our success to old-fashioned values and principles, those being preparation, hard work, integrity, loyalty, kindness, responsiveness, attention to detail, flexibility and a strong interest in continual improvement."

In light of such monumental — not to mention sizable — victories, I was curious to know what obstacles Shanin experienced as his firm grew. His answer was unusual in that he addressed a challenging issue not every business person will face: preconceived discrimination against his profession. "The public holds lawyers in low esteem, and they hold personal injury lawyers in especially low esteem. That translates to a potential issue in the courtroom with jurors. Of course, the jurors don't know us, and they don't know our firm, for the most part, so it can be difficult to get over those preconceived attitudes with jurors. What we have found to be successful is to be always candid with the jurors; to tell them the strong points and the weak points of our cases; to refuse to exaggerate the claims; to be straightforward and honest in every respect in the courtroom; and to win their confidence fair and square. Even with all of that, there will be some jurors whose negative feelings about the civil justice system will be so substantial that they may have a hard time reaching a fair verdict. But we have found that adhering to the guidelines I've described usually provides an outcome on the merits of the case. It usually produces an outcome on the merits, and not on some sort of collateral bias."

Aside from developing the guidelines Shanin described above — preparation, hard work, integrity, loyalty, kindness, responsiveness, attention to detail, flexibility and a strong interest in continual improvement — I wondered about other important leadership guidelines he developed during his illustrious career and how they have impacted his business.

"Always promoting the values that I've described. I think that as a law firm or other type of endeavor grows, there can be temptations to get out of your lane. That should be resisted, because when you get out of your lane you get out of an area with which you're familiar, and you can get chewed up in dozens of different ways through a lack of experience. We have tried hard, though not always successfully, to stay in our own lane."

I wondered if there were particular types of cases Shanin's firm tried that caused him to speak from experience. Indeed there were.

"There was a point in time 15 or so years ago where there was a developing shift in the tort liability field, potentially changing the laws that would apply to the claims in which we concentrate: the catastrophic injury claims, particularly in the area of medical malpractice. So we took a step into the class-action practice as a supplement to what we were doing. After five years of doing that, we found it to be unsatisfactory, and we reversed course. I learned it's easier to get into something than to get out of something, so that's an object lesson as well."

Shanin felt that his leadership structure in particular as well as the reasoning behind it would benefit readers. "The firm was founded by Tom Kline and me. We remain the only owners of the firm. A two-person ownership structure is very advantageous. The reasons that I say that are that a sole owner arrangement is very simple, but you need somebody to talk to, because with one person acting alone, that introduces a lot of fallibility into the dynamic of running an enterprise. Two very experienced people working together sharply reduces the risk of making a bad decision. There is a synergy with two experienced people working together that produces results far in excess of what those two people could produce if they were acting alone.

For that to work, obviously there has to be trust, and friendship, and mutual respect, and each partner needs to feel, and be committed, to the enterprise. There's an expression that you should try to do 60 percent of the work of the enterprise when you're in a two-person partnership, because your other partner won't see all the work you're doing, and I think that that's a good observation. I think Tom Kline and I work as hard as we possibly can for the success of our firm, and I think that's created a lot of mutual respect, and even harder work from each one of us. It's been a very, very good model.

The other aspect that I would point out is that in a two-person equal partnership, which is our arrangement, you have to have agreement. Because if one person says 'No', then the idea doesn't go forward. That's also a good thing. Sometimes one of us might be strongly in favor of something, and the other might be mildly opposed. The person who's mildly opposed will defer to the person who is strongly in favor, because of that mutuality of respect. On the other hand, if one person is strongly in favor and the other person is strongly opposed, or if one person is mildly in favor, and the other person is mildly opposed, then we don't go forward. That's probably saved us from a bunch of mistakes.

"We don't work the cases together, because we have too much work to do that. But in terms of making decisions (for example, about hiring particular new lawyers, or taking on a very large project such as a mass tort involving a defective product that may have caused a lot of people to be injured, which is going to commit the resources of a lot of people in the firm), we make them together."

When asking which books influenced Shanin in the way he conducts business, I learned something quite fascinating: he uses history to create closing speeches!

Shanin doesn't read a lot of the pop culture books. "I skip the self-help section of the bookstore, and some of the sections that are near the self-help section. I tend to rely on the lessons of history. I read a lot by and about Winston Churchill. That has been very useful to me. The way he guided the United Kingdom, particularly in 1940 when their backs were against the sea, literally, is inspirational and contains a lot of excellent lessons. The speeches that he gave in the House of Commons are great fodder for a closing speech in a courtroom, and also, they are great fodder for assessing what we want to achieve professionally. Professional satisfaction can be produced in many different ways, one of which is money, but there are other important ways as well, such as improving society."

If you haven't been privy to injury law on the level on which Shanin practices, you might not have considered before that the "wins" are about more than just monetary awards for their clients, but about the satisfaction of remedying the situation that caused the problem in the first place. How satisfying it must be to help so many!

Shanin said, "We have worked very hard in our cases to obtain remedies from the people that we sue that go beyond money, but include things such as changing their practices, changing the way they do business, changing the design of their products, changing the condition of their premises, changing hospital policies, changing police department procedures. That has been enormously professionally satisfying," Shanin explained. "It also to some degree, particularly where we live, has changed opinions about the importance of the work of trial lawyers. A lot of people who have come to understand our work have also come to understand the importance to themselves, and their family, and society, of the work of the trial bar in making our society safer."

I asked Shanin to discuss one of those significant moments in time when he was able to make a significant impact through his work in the community.

"Tom Kline recently settled a case against the City of Philadelphia involving a catastrophic injury sustained by an innocent civilian who was shot because of mistaken identity by plain-clothes police. In addition to maintaining a very large monetary recovery for the client, he got the police commissioner and city solicitor to agree to very significant changes to police procedures in the manner in which plain-clothes police officers identify themselves to suspects, so that suspects can know that they are dealing with a police officer and not with a robber. When somebody's coming at you with a gun and they're not wearing a police uniform, your assumption is going to be that that's not a police officer. You're going to flee. A young man was approached by men with weapons wearing plain-clothes, and he thought he was going to be robbed, and he sought to flee, and he was then shot because the officers didn't identify themselves. Tom's win resulted in a very important change in Philadelphia with the police department," he said.

"I had a case where on a clear sunny day a power line fell on top of a wife and mother in western Pennsylvania, causing her death by electrocution," Shanin said. "After a successful trial, I got the company to agree to inspect and fix all 26,000 miles of their power lines, and I got the public utility commission in Pennsylvania to change their procedures for the investigation of fatal incidents like this one in Pennsylvania. That's also a good thing, because all of us walk under power lines every day, and we're all at risk of an improperly installed or improperly maintained power line falling and killing us. Power lines fall with some frequency, even on a clear sunny day, but fortunately they don't tend to fall on top of people, but it can happen. It's certainly foreseeable that it will happen. Therefore, the power company needs to be sure that they've installed the lines correctly and that they inspect them."

Readers visiting www.klinespecter.com can click on the toolbar to view a drop-down menu for a synopsis of various cases in which the firm has achieved widespread remediation. Under "The Major Victories", you can read about money changing hands, but they have a whole different section of the website to talk about the kind of remediation Shanin has described above. "That's an important part of what we do, and we talk about it, and we think it's important to talk about it," he said in closing.

Shanin mentioned that determination, among other things, is what allowed him to succeed. I feel very strongly about the power of persistence and I was pleased to discover that many successful CEOs attribute perseverance as their No.1 factor to success. Let's take a closer look.

PART 3: PERSISTENCE

I'm convinced that about half of what separates the successful entrepreneurs from the non-successful is pure perseverance.
-Steve Jobs

Mention the name Steve Jobs to any business crowd and you'll likely hear all the usual descriptors in response: visionary, creative genius, tenacious, will of steel, dictatorial.

What is often not noted is the undeniable amount of perseverance Steve Jobs demonstrated to get to the place where most of us know of him best. While you may have heard that Steve Jobs was born to an unwed graduate student and given up for adoption, did you know the only stipulation his birth mother put forth was that her son be adopted by parents with college degrees?

So much for trying to control destiny: Jobs was adopted by two parents who not only did not have college degrees, but his father did not even have a high-school diploma! Jobs himself ended up dropping out of college when his parents could not afford to support his education. That pivotal point in his life could have been the end of a promising career. But it was only the beginning for Jobs.

He persevered by continuing to drop in on college courses (in other words, not paying) for another 18 months, where he discovered his passion for calligraphy. This would later translate to a passion for typefaces and would be channeled in his 1984 Macintosh computer. With Steve Wozniak, Jobs co-founded Apple in his parents' garage, only to be fired from his own company ten years later. In the 12-year interim before he returned to Apple, he founded NeXT and Pixar.

Once Jobs rejoined Apple, he was instrumental in bringing the company to the forefront of consumer electronics with iTunes and the iPod. Next Jobs would face his biggest challenge: a rare cancer (neuroendocrine tumor) diagnosis in 2004 when he was given 3-6 months to live.

In true Jobs fashion, he turned those few months into seven more years, utilizing hotly debated alternative medical treatments before finally agreeing to surgery. His employees often joked that around Jobs was a "reality distortion field" that allowed him to create his own reality in marketing his previously nonexistent products. Towards the end of his life, Jobs often discussed how he wanted to believe in the afterlife; that all the knowledge and experience one accumulates in life goes on. "I think it's just like an on-off switch. Click and you're gone. And that's why I don't like putting on-off switches on Apple devices."

I wondered how much of Steve Jobs's persistence the leaders I interviewed had. It turns out – a great deal!

Bob Ferris, VirTra

It's critical to communicate to every staff member why the company exists.

Did you know that eight out of ten entrepreneurs fail within the first 18 months, and only a third of businesses make it past their tenth anniversary? The more CEOs I interviewed, the more I wondered what it is that separates one out of five from the rest. I learned that you need to be very persistent, almost fanatical, in order to turn your vision into reality, like in the case of Bob Ferris, CEO of VirTra, Inc., which produces police judgmental use-of-force and de-escalation scenario training simulators.

Talk about pressure — the type faced by police every day... I was curious to learn more about this unique business.

Bob founded Ferris Productions, Inc. in 1993 and after the merger between Ferris Productions and GameCom in September 2001, he stepped down as CEO of the combined company, VirTra, until on May 22, 2008 he became the CEO once again but faced over $4 million in debt with just over $2 million in total revenue. Despite enormous adversity, Bob's vision was to create the most effective simulators in the world, and he helped create the ideas and attract the talent responsible for developing VirTra's market leading products. As one of the first virtual-reality-based companies in the world in 1993, their primary focus was and continues to be developing and delivering the world's most effective high-tech simulation systems. Bob and his team not only survived 2008 until today, but somehow, based on percentage growth in stock price from when they took over until today, an increase of 5,400 percent as of December 8, 2017, which outperformed two of the greatest companies of modern times: Amazon and Apple.

Given this incredible success, I was curious to know what Bob attributes his success to.

"The key factor I think would be grit, a belief that we'd eventually succeed, and the willingness to endure any amount of pain or setbacks. Like sprinting all out, even though you know it is a marathon, but as we neared the finish line it was pushed back, and then we'd get close to it, and it'd get pushed back again, and then pushed back again. That's how it felt during the second year in business! I refused to give up far beyond when a sensible person would rationally conclude it was obviously time to throw in the towel."

There is no question that the September 11 attacks changed the world. Bob was strongly inspired by the attacks to begin developing the world's most effective training simulator for first responders. Prior to 9/11, Bob's business had been focused around the Fortune 500 entertainment industry. The attacks caused Bob to change direction. Bob's team hit the reset button for the company, making the decision to create a brand-new line of products in a completely different market in the post-9/11 world. Bob said this was probably their biggest obstacle: to start-over the business from essentially scratch. Their vision was clear — to develop revolutionary new simulation training products that would impress the toughest police and military experts. VirTra had hard-earned experience in creating commercial simulators; they just lacked about everything else, such as money and customers. "What we did was to focus on making the best possible decisions at every step. We put the company ahead of ourselves. We were also abundantly persistent year after year, which returns to what I mentioned about grit. Out of our darkest moments came our most successful products that are now the gold standard for the industry and in daily use by the most respected police and military agencies around the world.

Bob's answer reminded me of that old question, "How do you eat an elephant?" Answer: "One bite at a time."

The lack of money and customers plus huge debts are very big hurdles to overcome when running a business. I wondered what Bob and his team did to survive, imagining their meetings trying to come up with a strategy to secure those crucial elements.

"As a team we had a willingness to persist. We would not give up, and were all determined to find a way," Bob explained. Their eventual success was not without what felt like miracles along the way. "At times we would get a critical break out of the blue. Once we were able to start selling the product in 2004, we would get a critical sale at the exact moment we most needed it. Many times it felt like manna from God, just enough to live another day."

Bob is far more comfortable talking about the talents, work ethic and importance of his coworkers than talking about himself. Bob's approach is that you show you care by action, not talk. Although years ago when the team was struggling to get the company off the ground, Bob explained they didn't have the money to provide 401(k) or health insurance benefits for their staff, but they were quick to provide those benefits the minute they could. "A healthy company is when the company truly cares about the workers in their business, and the employees truly care about the success of the business."

Echoing yet another commonality I'm discovering with successful CEOs, Bob mentioned the importance of communication. "I think it's critical to communicate to every staff member why the company exists. For VirTra, our 'why' is to save and improve lives through simulation training. Every three months, I hold a company-wide meeting in which I remind everyone why we exist as a company. We also update everyone on our progress in each department. We also go over our detailed financial results for the quarter during this meeting, and that's important because we provide profit share to our staff. One of our greatest challenges is to listen carefully to feedback from employees and customers with an open mind, and then correctly decide on what adjustments to make based on that new information."

Bob said that taking care of your people and caring enough for them to provide the best benefits you can is important. "Finding ways to make them truly feel they are a part of the company's bigger picture is crucial. For our business, exceptional employees are absolutely key to the long-term success of the company. A lot of companies treat people like they are just a number in a spreadsheet and I feel it's going to be very challenging for them to make it to 25 years, because staff turnover and losing your best staff can be utterly debilitating to a company's long-term success."

Like many top CEOs, Bob is an avid reader. "On average I read about a book per week; mostly books written by the leading experts in areas that are most relevant to the company at the time such as addressing our greatest challenges or our greatest opportunities. If the book is particularly impactful, I'll buy extra copies to give to our key staff members. I really believe that if you aren't learning from the top experts, you're already falling behind. But if I had to select the most impactful book for me, it would be when my son and I read together every night the Bible until, about three years later, we finished it."

VirTra is now publicly traded under the acronym "VTSI", so anyone can buy their stock today. To learn more about the company, visit www.virtra.com or go through the many sites that reference the company and its products. I'm delighted to say that I'm now working with Bob on his upcoming book which will be published by Leaders Press in early 2018.

Justin Tysdal, Seven Corners

Persistence is the key to our success.

Seven Corners, Inc. is an innovative and service-focused international travel insurance and specialty benefit management company. Their customers include international travelers, agencies of the U.S. government, foreign governments, corporations and various types of insurance companies. Seven Corners is privately held and strategically headquartered near Indianapolis in Carmel, Indiana.

In celebrating their quarter-century anniversary, I wanted to know the No.1 factor that CEO Justin Tysdal attributes to their success.

"I would say persistence. We've had a lot of challenges and there are many times in which we could have easily said, 'This is too much work.' Or 'It's not gonna work.' Or 'There's too many obstacles.' Or 'We don't know how the industry's gonna change.' Or 'All of our competitors are gone.' There were many times where we could have given up. Yet today we've doubled down and committed to ourselves to the next 25 years. I would say the biggest thing is just persistence is the one key factor for our success," Justin explained.

Keeping the doors open at Seven Corners was not without challenges. "When we first started out — maybe six months into the business — things weren't going quite right. We thought we would get a lot more business in the door, quite a bit more revenue. The expenses were higher than we thought they would be. We just looked at each other and asked, 'What do you want to do?'," Justin said. "And what we did was to get second jobs and keep at it. We kept doing what we thought was going to make sense in the long run. Within six months, or after about a year in business, things started to turn around where there was enough money coming in to keep the business going and we could afford to pay ourselves. Instead of working two jobs, we could just work the one. So, that's an example when we first started out. Over the years, we've had carriers, insurance companies, that have left the business; as well as some other people that have been interested in purchasing us. At each juncture we had to ask ourselves what we wanted to do. Each time we decided we didn't want to give up yet, we wanted to keep going."

Over the course of 25 years, Seven Corners faced some big obstacles. "The biggest obstacle was changing from a small company into a larger one; from a small business into a medium business. After 21 years in business, we knew we had to make a change, so we transitioned from an entrepreneur-led organization to a professionally managed business. We're three years into this evolution of our company, and we have a way to go," Justin said.

"Prior to this transition, we essentially ran our company like a small business where my partner and I were at the top of the organization. We were involved in the majority of the major decisions. Even though we had a management team in place, consisting of people with certain titles who had been around for a long time, they really weren't managing their departments the way that we needed them to," Justin said. "We had 200 people and yet we were still running the business like a small company. We started the process of changing the nature of the organization three years ago. We call it the Apollo program. We've learned a lot in three years, and have had a pretty good level of turnover. The executive members of the organization we have now are fantastic. They're everything that we dreamed they would be. Essentially, they're running most of the day-to-day business of the company rather than me and my partner.

We changed our culture from one that consisted of people used to receiving instructions, to a culture where we have people who are given opportunities and they come up with ways to devise their own solutions. Our new culture is more actively involved in the community," Justin explained. "For example, now we have a peer recognition program. We used to have something called 'Employee of the Month', where my partner and I chose an employee based on limited information, limited insight. It didn't work out at all. Now we have a peer recognition program where people recognize each other for living our core values or doing things in the best interest of our customers and that's working out great."

Considering the company's trajectory, I wondered if Justin has a long-term vision, and if is it different from the one he had when starting out.

Justin admits that when starting out, they had no idea where they were headed. "We thought we were going to be in business for a few years and then sell to a larger company. We thought everything that we knew was our own space in business, because international medical insurance is what we've always done. Since then, we've branched out from there, but initially our entire world was just focused around that industry, those producers, those insurance companies, those competitors."

The last several years opened their eyes to their true potential. "Now we're global, having expanded into Latin America where we offer the same type of solutions. The nature of insurance is changing and the old ways of buying insurance and servicing insurance are going by the wayside. It used to be that in order to file a claim, you had to contact your local agent and that person would start the process. Now you can start the process using an app on your phone. You take a picture of your car that was damaged or your house that was damaged and upload it into the system. Those sorts of changes in our industry, as well as the world, have opened our eyes to what the potential can be. Right now we're a $70 million company and our goal as a company is to grow tenfold in ten years, to a $700 million company."

Justin admits they're not quite sure of the path. "We know that it's an audacious, ambitious goal to grow ten times in ten years, but we honestly believe that we've got the people on board as well as people coming on board in the near future that could figure out that path. So many of our competitors have sold out to larger insurance companies or other organizations. We want to turn ourselves into one of those organizations that continues to grow and expand beyond what we thought we would do 24 years ago."

With such a monumental goal, I asked Justin how he will find the right people to help them fulfill their ambition.

He said during the selection process, they look for those who share their vision and have an absolute deep desire to be part of it. "The biggest things we can do as a company is to give the best work environment to our team members, as well as the opportunity to do amazing things. We feel we've got the platform and the opportunity for people to come on board and be great. We just have to make sure we can sort through the process to find the right people.

It's difficult. We might find somebody whose only

experience is growing 3 percent to 4 percent a year in their particular line of business when we're looking for 30 percent year-over-year growth," Justin said. "We have to find the right person; someone that has not only the desire, but the experience. Within our space, it really hasn't happened before. International medical and travel insurance is a pretty steady growth type business, so we have to find people who think outside the box and are not afraid to have a work experience where there's pretty significant change each and every year."

I asked Justin what types of questions he might ask to see if potential recruits will be able to make his vision happen.

"We go through, depending on the role specifically, a traditional multi-process interview that's an hour long. Questions can include past experience. 'What are the driving forces in your life? What are you motivated by?' Then we come at it from a different angle where we ask the candidate to present a plan for their first 90 days. We ask them what the first 90 days look like. We also ask, 'What do the first 180 days look like? What does the first year look like?' We want to see how they think; to get a sense as to how they think about things. Whether it's just an academic presentation or whether it's an infused presentation based on past experience or their own experience, a little bit about what they know about the company so far, a little bit of research and investigation into the industry." By that point in time, they feel they have a good idea as to whether there's a level of commitment there, as well as a level of ability.

I wanted to know if Justin had developed any laws of leadership that were written down or put on the wall.

Most of their values were developed during the past three years. "Before that, we were a small company. Things weren't functioning properly. We weren't happy with the sort of work that we were doing as an organization. The core values are now on the wall. For me, it's not necessarily anything that's written down, but the overall theme that I have is to provide great people with a great work environment and then challenging experiences and to let them do great things on their own. Some of the people that have recently come on board know that it's going to be a challenge, that the information isn't readily available, that the system needs certain changes. But they are the ones absolutely thirsting for that sort of an experience. As CEO, it's important for me to make sure I can create that environment where it's not only great but also that it's in a space with potential for them to develop exactly how we're going to get to 10 times in 10 years.

As I said before, I don't have a path there yet. If we do A, B and C, we're going to grow 30 percent a year and then we're going to get to a $700 million company. I have no idea how we're going to get there. I know that there's a lot of opportunity in the international insurance market. I know that insurance in general is going through a lot of changes. And I know that if I find the right people and give them somewhat of a vision and then give them the ability and the authority to make the right decisions, then we'll figure out some way to get there. I approach it at my level in looking at the overall health of the organization rather than any particular set of direct, specific instructions."

I find Justin's goal of growth to be fascinating. To understand the challenge before him, I asked about his growth in the last 10 years.

He said the company is doing well, and they are already used to that type of growth. "Sometimes it was 10 percent, sometimes it was 20 percent, but that was a good rough figure. For the last three years, we've been investing in our systems, and getting ready for the next phase of growth. We were doing well before. 30 percent every year is definitely ambitious, but we absolutely believe it's possible."

Justin feels it's important to have a somewhat audacious goal. "Because if you're trying to build an organization of people who want to do amazing things, 5 percent year-over-year is not necessarily a great magnet for them. If you're going to be in business, and you want to make an impact on the industry and the people that work here, you've got to set an impressive target and then work as a team on figuring out how to get there. The small target just doesn't work.

Because our industry had been changing, everybody that we were competing against 24 years ago has now been sold to somebody else. The organizations exist, the brand could still exist, but essentially, they're owned by a larger organization. As a company, to be able to do well, we couldn't stay small anymore. We had to grow at a rate that would be able to support our organization as it goes up against those larger companies," Justin said.

When Justin said the small targets aren't effective, I am reminded of the quote, "Aim for the moon and you might land among the stars." Next, I was curious to know which books have influenced Justin and the way he conducts business.

"The one that in the last three years has been the most consistent is a book called *Traction* by Gino Wickman," Justin said. "The author took, I think, pieces from four different business books and created something that was easy to digest and easy to understand. Traction is what he's describing as an entrepreneur's operating system with a series of meetings, accountability chart, organizational structure, talent evaluation. It's an easy read, but then it's also a very good foundation for establishing good habits. We started using it three years ago. We're using it less now as we've brought more people on board and we're not an entrepreneur's organization anymore, but that's been the most impactful book.

I also think *Great by Choice* by Jim Collins and Morten T. Hansen is terrific. It helps lay out the 30 percent year-over-year vision and how to make that possible with a lot of common sense. I'm reading a book right now called *Radical Candor* by Kim Scott that is about how to give people feedback and why it's important; the people that work in your organization as well as your organization itself. I'd say those three are probably, off the top of my head, the most influential." When Justin finds a book he feels is impactful, he shares it with his team. "Sometimes I give everybody copies. Other times I roll it out to a couple of people in order to get some immediate feedback to see if it's applicable, and then I start buying copies."

To learn more about Seven Corners, you can visit www.sevencorners.com or find Justin Tysdal on LinkedIn.

Ron Peri, Radixx International

Become convinced that you can't fail.

Ron Peri has 30 years' experience in information technology and architected the first major replacement of an IBM mainframe with PC networks in 1987. His replacement of an IBM 3090 mainframe with PC technology reduced annual IT operating expenses by more than 90 percent at the reinsurance division of Beneficial Life Insurance (subsequently spun out as American Centennial Insurance, Inc.) and made front-page news in *The Wall Street Journal* as the "vanguard of a revolution." Radixx International, Inc. is an industry-leading provider of travel distribution and passenger service system software for airline reservations, distribution and merchandising.

Radixx is now delivering its sixth-generation passenger service system. Founded in 1993 and now hosting 50 airlines on six continents, Radixx's fully integrated, cloud-based solutions support all airline business models.

When I asked Ron what he attributes his success to, he explained that there are two factors. "One has to do with a person's character, and the other with the way they approach the business. The first, I would say, is perseverance, and in my specific case, is driven by faith in God. The second is managing cash. The single most important factor for making it in business is becoming convinced that you can't fail. It's persevering through the hard times and not giving up, always keeping your eye on the cash."

Ron believes there is always a way forward. "My brother, who has worked with us as our attorney over the years, has a saying, 'You just need to live to fight again another day.' In other words, it's the idea that you're continuing to kick the can down the road. As you're falling over, put your foot out in front of you so that you just keep from failing today. Many times over the years people advised me to give up. In fact, dozens of times, at least dozens. I always believed we would find a way forward. I think optimism is the key ingredient in perseverance and I've always been an optimist. I'll give you an example. We had just lost our largest client who was responsible for 30 percent of our business. It was 2008, several of our investors and board members had lost a lot in the market, and as I sat with our board and reviewed the situation, they felt we should shut down the business.

They said, 'Look, Ron, you've run a good race; you've worked harder and accomplished more than we ever could have expected.' But they were convinced that this was the end. I vehemently disagreed, and I refused to give up. I convinced them that I could make a go of it.

They said, 'Okay, but we're not going to put any more money in the business.' A few months later, everything started to turn around, and we began to turn a modest profit. Within four years, we were regularly winning new airline business and very profitable," Ron said.

"A few weeks after that board meeting, as I was looking for other sources of cash, I visited a very successful entrepreneur.

He was very wealthy and very successful. After reviewing our financials and our business model, his advice was, 'Ron, you've got a great product; you've got a great business model. Take the company into bankruptcy, and buy it out again at a bargain price. You're effectively bankrupt right now. After that, come and talk with me and I can help you.' Well, I couldn't do that because I had about 20 small investors who would have suffered, and who would have lost everything they'd invested. I didn't want to take advantage of them," Ron said.

There's a fiduciary responsibility that an owner has to the investors, and to the employees, and to the clients. "I told the investor I was convinced that the product we were building was going to change the industry. But we were funding the development out of our own operations, and it was going to take a few years before we would see significant financial success. That's exactly what eventually happened. I never took in an investment from him."

On one occasion, Ron lost courage and thought Radixx was finished. "It was New Year's Eve about 15 years ago, maybe 2002. I was sitting in my office, and I was considering what I could do to make the payroll, because we were going to have another shortfall. Part of my challenge then was always figuring out how to cover payroll. It was twice a month, and throughout most of the 25 years that was a challenge, until the last few years. This time though it was much worse, because I needed $157,000 on the next business day, which would've been January 2. I was there in the office and it was about 3 in the afternoon and everybody else had left for the holiday, except for our vice president who was there with me.

As I thought about it, there was only one possible source of funds, but it was far short of our need of $157,000. A few weeks earlier, I had received a court document regarding a client who had gone bankrupt several years prior and they were promising us a partial payment of our claim within the next month in the amount of approximately $42,000, which was not nearly enough, and I didn't know if it was going to arrive in time. There was nowhere else that I could get money for payroll. Shortly after that, I looked up and the vice president walked into my office with a FedEx letter, and he said, 'Ron, I think you'll want to see this.' He hadn't opened it, but it was from the bankruptcy courts," Ron said.

He opened the envelope, figuring it would contain a check for $42,000 that would flutter out. "Instead, I looked at the check, and it was a check for $157,000. Exactly what I needed! Now, I had been sitting in my office praying — thanking God for the provision of the past years, praying for his guidance in handling this crisis, asking for strength, for wisdom to handle whatever came next, praying for protection for employees, customers and vendors, and it was in the midst of that praying that this fellow walked in. Now we had a lot of little miracles like that that worked together to strengthen both my faith, and that of others at Radixx. We pulled together as a team, and persevered. People knew our situation; we didn't hide it from them. It was a joint effort. I have a whole lot more stories like that, but that one is particularly appropriate, just because people understand cash. To get the precise amount of cash — it wasn't $156,000 — it was $157,000, exactly what we needed."

One of the biggest obstacles Ron has faced many times was around cash flow. "It was lack of cash many times. We had to have a close relationship with the bank. I started my first business capitalized with $500 and gave it a big name, Computer Support North America, but it was really Ron Peri with a desk in the basement of my home, behind the furnace, with a phone and a business card. Three years later, that company was on the front page of *The Wall Street Journal*. A few years after that, we sold that, for a significant amount, to a New York Stock Exchange listed company. The deal was back-ended. I got a portion of the sale price at closing, which was a life-changing amount. When they went bankrupt two years later, however, I was their largest unsecured creditor," Ron said.

He went on to start the company that ultimately became Radixx. "But this time I started with $200,000, and again we were severely undercapitalized for what we were trying to do. We compensated for the lack of cash — and this is the first thing — if you don't have enough cash, it requires sweat equity. We put in a great deal of sweat equity. Just hard work, fewer people than we would've liked to have hired and everyone had multiple jobs and they were on the go, traveling worldwide. As CEO, I could just as well be doing a small building repair or flying halfway around the world to meet a client on short notice, and working sometimes 10, 12, 14 days in a row; many of our people were doing it as well. My approach to management is very personal, and I think that has helped. Our people are very loyal, very hardworking, very committed. We approach things as a team, and maybe even beyond that, I would say as a family; we worked through the issues together.

We weren't always in compliance with our loan terms at the bank and we were very honest with the bank; we never tried to cover and were very transparent. I think that transparency, by the way, is key to a good banking relationship. When we couldn't meet payroll, I would drive to the bank wearing my best suit, sit down with the vice president, and I would advise him about our precise situation. I would tell him exactly which clients would be paying, how much, and when I would be able to cover the shortfall. Then they would work with us. We would jointly find a way to cover payroll, whether it was a very short-term note, or whether it was carrying a negative balance for a few days. There was a variety of different ways they helped us. Some of those approaches would not work today, with some changes in the banking laws, but nonetheless, just being very transparent with the bank made us partners because if a bank lends you money, they have a vested interest in seeing you get through the hard time. They don't want to lose their money, they don't want to write off that note, and they don't want to go through the painful process of trying to collect money from a failed company," Ron explained.

He admits it wasn't the most pleasant way to do things. "We managed to get through each of those situations. Sometimes it was speaking with one of our board members or investor, or even friends. I would just tell people the situation I was dealing with. I remember I called one fellow who was over 80 years old. He had been an entrepreneur for years and I told him, 'Look, I'm struggling to make payroll. I need to come up with about $60,000. What would you suggest?' I really was just asking for advice, but he said, 'Ron, I'll wire you $100,000. You'll have it in your bank by this afternoon.'

The arrangement we worked out was that he would get interest at a hefty rate. He wound up going to a nursing home and his son told me that his father had made some pretty bad investments, and that the monthly amount that we had been paying him enabled him to stay in the nursing home and to have the money he needed at that point in his life," Ron said.

"Persevering and believing that there is a way forward may not make itself obvious. A lot of it is overcoming the obstacles," Ron said. "For me anyway, it meant a lot of time praying, and I would be very specific and write down what I was praying about. It was kind of interesting, because after some years I could go back and look and see all the specific things that had happened, and I believe in response to my prayers, and it was like an experimenter's journal, I could see what happened over time. That tended to build faith, and I do think that starting and running an under-capitalized company builds your faith, either in God or in yourself. For some people, God's not part of the equation, so they've got to come up with a solution on their own, I suppose. For me, it's strength in my faith in God. Then I had a great group of friends and investors. I got a lot of encouragement from them. Sometimes I got some money to assist, and for all of them, anybody who invested in Radixx, they made many, many times their original investment. We took in very little money," Ron said.

I have heard many times that it's important to nurture relationships with other small business owners and entrepreneurs in order to have a mutual support network. Even if it's not money, it could just be advice. Ron agreed. "Absolutely. I would go to other entrepreneurs, and seek advice. There are a few of them that I would call and sometimes they would call me, and we would discuss how to handle some particular situations.

Another major obstacle that we had to deal with was dealing with other cultures. We went international fairly quickly about 18 years ago, initially in Africa, and then subsequently in Asia, on the Indian subcontinent to begin with. We quickly learned that in the developing world a contract means something different than it does in the States," Ron explained. "Here it's based on trust; you trust one another, you each make commitments, and you write it down so that you can remember what you have committed to, because it's easy to forget the details at a later date. Elsewhere, it's based on a lack of trust: I'm gonna use this to hold you to do whatever I can stretch this to mean." Ron has coined a saying when doing business in the developing world: "a signed contract is the beginning of negotiations". He explains, "Now, this is very different from what you encounter in the U.S., where generally speaking, if you have a signed contract, you have established the terms of your business relationship, and people operate by those terms."

I know that Radixx recently received a major investment, and Ron became the chairman, and brought in a CEO. I asked about the big changes at the company.

"I would say, without trying to rank them, one factor was the fact that we had people who had invested 20+ years ago, and had never seen a dime. We never paid a dividend, and so the only opportunity for them to get any return on their investment was either if we were to sell the company or take in a very large investor who bought them out. We had actually lost two of our core investors when they died," Ron said.

"A second thing is that I've been doing this for a long time. I've spent 35 years now as an entrepreneur, and I had another company before this. It just seemed like it was time. Plus, I was getting calls on a daily basis from private equity firms and others wanting either to invest in or acquire the company. Shakespeare has an interesting quote: 'There is a tide in the affairs of men, which, taken at the flood, leads on to fortune.' It continues on to say that if you miss it, it's gone. Some of it was recognizing that it was the appropriate time: there was an opportunity, there were people who were interested, and we had a lot of people who had that need."

Ron recognized his own strengths and weaknesses.

"Having done this for almost a quarter of a century, I realized that although we had a great product, for us to scale the company, I didn't have all the skills necessary to take it to the next level. That wasn't a painful thing for me to realize; it's just realistic. There are certain things that I can do very well. For other things we needed someone else. We had been preparing to have an investment banker represent the company either in a sale or a significant investment. As I would get these calls from private equity firms, I would say,

'In several months, we're going to put out a package and we'll include you.' We had about a dozen different fairly substantial private equity firms that were interested. Then, we got a preemptive bid, and it was substantial and it was enough, so the investors said to go with this offer. They had more to offer than just money, which was a key factor. They've really helped us to find a new CEO, and the fellow we have is phenomenal, well beyond anything I could've hoped for," Ron said.

I respect the integrity that Ron has kept in Radixx. It seems that recognizing your own limitations, and delegation to others, is a big part of leadership.

Ron agreed. "I also think that integrity is core, which leads me to the laws of leadership I have developed. I believe in operating with absolute integrity and transparency. For example, I would sit down with a client and say, 'Look, here's the situation. It's not one that makes me happy or you happy, but this is what it is.' If people know that you keep your word, they will deal with you even through the hard times. It's not at all uncommon, and we run into it, that people will fudge a little bit or even lie in order to move things forward."

Ron has encountered that a few times with people he's hired. "I sit down and do a little intervention. If they don't buy into that and their character continues to manifest itself in a negative way, then we release them. That's hard, but it's kind of tough to keep somebody who lies because then you don't know where you are. You never know what really is true and what is not, and the bottom line is you really can't manage if you don't have good information.

As I said, it's important to operate with absolute integrity and transparency. I started my career with IBM, and I had several clients that went bankrupt. I remember one initially that was failing and there was a total change in the personality of their CEO. He was lying; he began cheating; he began doing things differently just to try to survive." Ron said. "I realized I never wanted to be like that. Certainly, money, or lack of money, and a desperate need to come up with money can bring out the worst in some people. I believe that it was just more important to maintain base integrity and then whatever happens, happens.

Then I would have responsibilities to the employees, and investors, and customers to deal with the best that I could. I feel a second law of leadership would be to care for your employees as if they were your own family. For example, the first company we sold was a decent sized company. The company we sold to did not have that attitude, and had little concern for their people. I can remember sitting around at an executive meeting and the CEO said, 'We gotta kill 20 people.' Meaning, we have to lay off 20 people.

He just saw those people as numbers. That was it: they had a salary and that was cost, and they had to go. I view it very differently. I think that if you take an interest in your people, and you effectively shepherd them — it's the servant/ leadership model; you encourage them at every turn. I will talk with our folks about their families, about their life struggles, sometimes finding out that somebody has a special need. Some unique situation happened in their lives, and to the degree we've been able to help, whether it's been money or otherwise, we have. That engenders great loyalty, and what we've seen is that people work far beyond what we could ever pay them to do, because there's such a strong sense of family. For many, many years I would stop by every desk in the morning and spend a few minutes with as many people as I could. I worked hard to break down the idea that some people arrived with that there is management and then there's everybody else," Ron said.

"We're a team here, we're a family, we're a group of people working together, and everybody's got to work. You're going to spend more time with the people at work than anywhere else. I want everybody to be approachable and available regardless of their level in the company; that includes me. That has helped tremendously. Ultimately, a key to success is productivity. It's not the only one, but it's a key to success. People are much more productive if they believe they're appreciated; if they believe you care about them; if they believe that you will reward them to the degree that you can. I think they're also quite understanding. If you run into a problem and you have a good relationship, I think that a group of people can overcome almost anything."

Naturally, I was curious about which books have influenced Ron the most.

"I would say the Book of Proverbs. The Bible generally, but specifically, the Book of Proverbs. It is ancient wisdom that is applicable today, because it deals with how human beings actually behave. I have found that to be extremely helpful. The other book that I found helpful is *Blue Ocean Strategy* by W. Chan Kim and Renée Mauborgne. The basic concept is that if you're competing where everybody is competing, then that is very much like the sharks all trying to eat from the same small group of fish. The ocean becomes red with blood. If, however, you're off doing something where you don't have that kind of competition then the ocean is blue. The idea is to look for ways to sell your product where it is blue ocean; where you don't have as much competition. It's not always a different product. It could be the same product as others, but maybe you could sell it differently.

For example, in our industry, everyone historically has charged a fee, a transaction fee, and we departed from that with a couple of our clients, and licensed the software with a one-time license fee and maintenance. It's not that original, but it's very different from the way our competitors were handling things, and that provided both our airline clients, and Radixx with significant financial benefit," Ron said.

Ron also likes *The One Minute Manager* by Ken Blanchard and Spencer Johnson. "It's an outstanding book. There's a key management technique that fits well with my management style which is if you have bad news or criticism that you have to present to an employee, begin with something very positive that they have done. Then share whatever the news is, or whatever you have to tell them, and then conclude with something positive. Also, do it in minutes, not a two-hour meeting. And address the individual items as individual items so that somebody doesn't think you're just unloading on them."

Ron was the first CEO to ask me if I had any advice for him. He was also curious to learn if there were commonalities between his interview and the other leaders. I said there have been some similarities which I've noticed, like keeping your people invested, and having transparency in business dealings. There have also been some great differences too in gaining an interesting insight into the various ways of building a company and nurturing that company to success.

I was excited to learn that not only is Ron considering writing a book but he already has a working title. "Our new CEO said, 'Ron, you've got to capture this and write it down.' "

"I shared one little miracle with you about the last-minute check for $157,000, but there are 25 years of miracles. We are the little engine who could. When the European Commission had to analyze the acquisition of one of our competitors by another larger one, they first had to determine who were the major players in the industry. There turned out to be six — now five because one got acquired. There were four others, all multi-billion-dollar companies, and then there was our little company, and we're a lot smaller than that.

We provide airline reservation hosting services, and it's all extremely mission-critical. We enable sales, check-in and distribution of everything an airline sells. The system can't be down. If it's down, then nobody can buy anything, nobody can check in for flights, no one can make a change. It's a high-pressure type of environment. There have been multiple failed attempts to try to build these kinds of systems by some of the largest companies in the world. We've been successful. We didn't do it as a big company would, as a massive multi-year project. We didn't say "We are going to set out over the next four years, spend a couple hundred million bucks, and build this new whizbang system," Ron said. "We just built it incrementally. We started with one little airline, a start-up at that point, and then just continued adding other airlines over the years until we got to where we are now," Ron said.

To learn more about Ron Peri, you can visit LinkedIn, www.radixx.com or Ron's website at ronperi.net.

Scott Fairley, CheckPoint Pumps & Systems

Set goals and keep going.

CheckPoint Pumps & Systems is a leading provider of chemical injection solutions. They design, manufacture and market arguably the world's most reliable chemical injection pumps, pump packages, control panels, pressure test systems, green energy solutions, and process components.

I asked Scott Fairley, CheckPoint's president, what he considers to be the No.1 factor behind his company's success. "Our success comes from realizing our goals, and you can't realize your goals without passion. I never started on this path for the money. I have always believed that if you are successful in creating passion and realizing your goals, the rewards — whatever they may be — will naturally follow. I started this journey so that I could wake up on a Monday morning and be excited. It's the greatest tragedy when someone spends their life dreading work; after all, we spend so much of our precious time working. If you can be passionate about work, you will be passionate about life. So you start with passion and then you set goals. You always have to have goals and you have to focus on those goals no matter what," Scott said.

Scott said his team is unwavering when they set a goal. "Every step of our 25-year journey has been a march toward a goal. To achieve goals, you have to move and adapt quickly. Procrastination is the absolute enemy of success. I impose that on anyone who will listen, 'There is no such thing as a bad or a good decision, there are only good and bad results. It's what we do with those results that will define us and strengthen our resolve to achieve our goals.' The only exception to that rule is procrastination — making no decision at all. That's a bad decision no matter the result. Lastly, and most importantly, is your team. The greatest asset I have is my team. I have spent the best part of 25 years finding a team that is as passionate about CheckPoint as I am and I now have that team. I would urge any entrepreneur to tattoo on their hand: 'As you grow, surround yourself with great people.' When it's just you, you have 100 percent passion in your company, when you have 99 employees, there may be only 1 percent passion. Employ well, give direction, mentor and build passion in your company; it's the difference between success and failure. Never forget, everything you do is for one purpose, and that is to satisfy your client. Your team will one day be the product or the service that your client interacts with. Clients can feel the good, the bad, and the ugly of the people they are dealing with — and that is the face of your company," Scott said.

He feels it's crucial for a company to set goals and keep going, even while there are multiple things going on at once. "You're building up your team, you're setting goals and then you're having your team focus on those goals. I know friends who have owned businesses, some successful, some unsuccessful. When I speak to them or they come to me for advice — whether it's a start-up or they're going through a crisis stage — I see that a lot of companies lose focus. To me that's their biggest problem. I always start with their team. You've got to pick a team that's as passionate as you are in pursuing and focusing on the goals of the company," Scott said.

At the same time, Scott advised that whilst pursuing your goals, you don't take your eye off why you're in business. "Over time, a lot of companies start becoming very insular. They look too intensely at what the company is doing internally and get lost in details that don't ultimately help the customer ('What color are the walls?', 'Is our logo perfect?', 'Is our marketing perfect?', Redesigning products that work great)," Scott said. "You've got to stop being so insular and focus on what your customers want. Because all of this is pointless if your customers are not being serviced and don't want to come back and work with you. Your goals have got to be very customer-focused.

I find that sometimes you get too bogged down in the pursuit of perfection and the result is that plans don't get implemented in a timely manner. It's okay to get 80 percent towards your goal and then set new goals. Of course, you've got to be sure to complete things but you don't have to get to 100 percent all the time. Many people that I work with, they want to thrash out a problem until it's 100 percent solved," Scott said. "I feel strongly that if you can get yourself to 80 percent, then you implement. You've got to implement because you don't know how something's going to work successfully or unsuccessfully without trying it, without making it live.

Once you start with a problem or a goal, it's easy to sidetrack on all the chain events that getting to that goal will cause. Then you start trying to solve for every eventuality, and you can't. You end up in meeting after meeting, and a plan that should have taken three months ends up being uncompleted nine months down the road. And you're no further toward your goal because you're so caught in the weeds that you forget what your actual goal was, and sometimes you just have to say, 'This isn't perfect; let's implement it'," Scott said.

Scott maintains there is no such thing as perfect. "Even if you could create perfect, it's going to be imperfect tomorrow because the dynamics of any business are changing constantly. If you think you're going to put black-and-white plans in place, you've got to think again. You've got to learn how to use an eraser pretty quickly. As companies grow, they experience larger, more complex problems. You've got to learn to wind yourself back and execute. You need to get it done and then you can massage, and adjust, and move it. But if you procrastinate, if you don't make decisions, nothing's going to happen. You'll have 100 percent of nothing, or you can have 80 percent of something that you can work with. You've got to start somewhere."

Considering Scott's adage to get to 80 percent, I was curious to know if he could remember his very first goals 25 years ago and how he experienced meeting his goals. He explained that when the original partners developed and patented their product, their first goal was to get the pumps — the main product — out on trial, and get them in the customer's hand. "When I started our U.K. operation, I remember thinking at the time that this was going to be an impossible task. We sat down and decided that the best way was to give our products free to customers as we had done in the U.S. As salesmen, it's our job to say that we've got the best product, but we needed to let our product speak for itself directly to the customer. We needed to get customer feedback and see if they loved it as much as we did," Scott explained.

"We achieved that fairly quickly and then set our next goal, selling the product. All baby steps, but well planned and executed. And we didn't think 25 years in advance when we started the business; we were thinking day to day, week to week. I guess that's another piece of advice. I deal a lot with investment companies and banks who are interested in working with us. They want five-year plans and ten-year plans, and all this information. And the fact is when you have a small privately-owned business, you don't plan five years in advance and ten years in advance, and set goals for that because it's almost impossible. You certainly have to look at the future, but the detail should be in the present," Scott said.

"We're in the business of oil and gas, a traded commodity. There are multiple factors that influence our market — politics, geography, wars. The list is long and it is almost all out of our control. You can't plan for what the oil price is going to be. We can only plan for what we can influence. Of course, I still think about where I'd like the company to be in the future, but I don't always share that with all of my team. I feel that that distracts them from the short-term goals. I'll worry about the long-term goals, they worry about the short-term." Scott sets big goals for himself and then multiple small goals for his team, and they have fun trying to guess his ultimate goal.

I asked Scott what he considered a healthy goal progression for a CEO who's just starting out and trying to ramp up their business. He said it starts with getting the right employees from the beginning. "When you first start a business, you are not thinking about your employment needs; you are thinking about what you're doing to survive. Before you know it, you're employing people; it's surprising how quickly it happens. One of the most important goals at that stage is to spend time and energy picking the right people from Day 1. You are so busy with your growing business, you neglect to spend the time picking exceptional employees.

We often hired in a state of emergency; we needed to fill a

gap quickly. I wish we had planned more and spent more energy interviewing the staff and understanding what their long-term goals were, and how they would fit into our philosophy and vision of the company in the future. It would have saved us a lot of time and energy had we done that at the beginning," Scott explained.

I then asked Scott to tell me one of the biggest obstacles his company had to overcome in those 25 years and how he overcame it. "When we got to a certain size, somewhere between small and medium, there was a chance we could stagnate, get lost in a comfortable no man's land. We struggled at that point. We could be a very successful 'lifestyle' business or we could push onward and continue to grow.

The company had a core base of customers who were always going to buy enough product to give them that comfortable lifestyle. But we were at the mercy of the markets as to whether we grew or shrunk that month, that quarter, or that year. We were in danger of losing control of our success. Also, as I said, I started all of this because I wanted to wake up on a Monday morning and be excited about the week ahead of me and I found I'd lost that excitement a little bit. I was enjoying the fruits of our labor but not really challenging myself, and not having the passion that I once had. The company was on autopilot. When my partner, and original founder of CheckPoint, Andy Elliott and I sat down together, we said, 'Why should we stop here? It's comfortable, but we never started this to be in a comfortable zone.'

We deliberated about it a lot because when CheckPoint started, it was a relatively small amount of money that was invested." Scott said. "The risk was minimal, we were young and had it not worked out we could have pursued other careers. Our biggest fear now was what we could lose. We had over 100 employees that had families counting on their meal on the table every evening coming from CheckPoint's success. We had a lot more time and money invested in it. Looking back, we'd spent over a decade traveling away from our families and being locked in our offices for 18 hours a day building the business. We'd invested a lot of our lives, so to think that we could make decisions that could harm the company and the employee was very scary," Scott confessed. "My other fear was that we had gathered an amazing, young executive team and sooner or later they were going to start recognizing the stagnation. It wouldn't be long before they would be looking for more exciting challenges. I didn't want to lose them. They came to us because they saw the passion and growth potential in the company and themselves.

I knew the statistics about start-ups and ten-year companies and so forth. We had no interest in selling the business in any way, shape, or form and we had made it this far. We re-evaluated everything and set even more aggressive goals. I had to reignite the passion and get ready for the next phase. It was like starting again. I refocused," Scott said.

Scott and his executive team went on to make a lot of bold changes that redefined their company and culture. "We made these changes with conviction and a certainty that we could adapt and make it to the next stage of our development, as we had learnt well from our early years. A new problem arose, however, during this transitional period. It occurred to me that we were concentrating our energies on CheckPoint internally and were in danger of losing focus on why we were doing all of this, which was to supply our clients with the best product available to them. I put trust in a few members of my team and had them concentrate on the detail of how the company could and would work daily, whilst I stayed at the 50,000 viewpoint and made sure that the end result was true to our company's values.

This taught me a valuable lesson: about 90 percent of the

work that CheckPoint actually does day to day, I cannot do. I am not a machinist, design engineer, accountant or mechanic. I don't need to be as I employ great people who are. My job is to make sure that those great people, as a group, achieve CheckPoint's goals. I am the conductor, not the musician. I delegate and trust, and I remind myself of this every day," Scott said.

There were a lot of factors that played into Scott's decision to push forward. "Honestly, it was the best decision we'd ever made. Looking back, it's easy to see, but the things that we worried about didn't become a problem. We did what we always did: we set goals and plans to reach those goals, we moved forward with conviction and passion and our employees recognized this and so they all dug deeper and went that extra mile. We were back at full speed. We all had something to invest again, whether it was time, money, shares. They saw direction and progression. They saw they had a career potentially for life, so everyone worked a little bit harder. It was a great decision, but we certainly had a lot of fear at the time," Scott said.

"When a company makes it to a certain age, there are certain milestones that dictate where the company is going to go next. The older the company gets, it can get a little bit more clouded by comfort decisions. You certainly don't want to be reckless, but you've always got to come back to the question of how you got here and recognize that that was by moving. It wasn't by sitting and waiting; it was by moving. It's rarely a bad idea to move forward, especially if you've successfully done it for as long as you have. That's not luck; that's skill, passion, devotion, dedication. You carry on with that secret source, that ingredient. You're going to be successful going forward as long as your market hasn't changed," Scott said.

"I'm a true believer in the importance of passion. I can still feel the passion for my business when I talk about it. 25 years later I still get excited about our little company. It's something that I'm proud of, and the passion is still very much there and I think that as long as that's there, anything else is achievable. As long as you're passionate, and you look forward to it, and you want to do it every day, I think the results just come from that passion. And once you get to a certain size, you have a team — and that team is hugely important. You have to have a team that's as passionate as you are.

On its own that's a challenge, because I'm certainly passionate about the company. I've been there from the early days. I've seen it grow. I've seen it shrink. I've seen it in great times and in bad times. Keeping a great team and keeping them passionate has been a challenge. How do you do that? My decision over the years has been to let my team invest in the company. That investment can take many forms other than the traditional business meaning. We invest in them and they invest in us. They feel that they're doing it for the company, which in turn rewards them. As I've said, your team is probably without exception the most important thing you can have. If you get a passionate team together, you can't fail," Scott said.

Persistence is really self-explanatory: you've got to keep going. "There are so many companies that set goals and stop pursuing them. If you've got to where you are, you're good at setting goals, and your goals probably have very good reasons to be set. Don't stop pursuing them! There are going to be obstacles. There's going to be fear. There are going to be market changes. But pursue your goals, at least to the point where you know it's a no-brainer to stop pursuing them.

An important lesson I've learned over the years is not to let pride get in your way of recognizing that you've spent money and time and energy, gotten to 80 percent and implemented, but it's just not going to work. You've got to know when to stop and set a new goal. Don't stop and mope about the decision that you made. Instead, ask what you have learned from getting to 80 percent of your goal? Create a new goal from that. Figure out how to make it work going forward through learning from what you've just done.

And don't be scared to change things up," Scott advised. "It's easy to stick to what you're doing but that has a finite life.

You have to keep adapting, and changing, and diversifying. That's what we've done throughout the years. We've opened up overseas offices — very challenging to do. Vertical integration, taking control of some of our supply chain, reducing costs and keeping control of deliveries and quality — at the time, all of these decisions were scary. We spent a lot of time and money on these projects but they have all paid off and have made the business stronger and better.

Scott said the trick is to make a plan, set a goal, hit it, and make it work for you. "All these things we did kept the business within our control; kept the cost within our control. With the overseas diversification, as one market goes down, another market goes up. Right now we're looking at diversifying into a more industrial market and trying to take some of our business out of the oil and gas because we've just gone through three years of hell with oil prices and inconsistencies. Again we sat down and asked ourselves, 'How do we solve this?'

Our pumps are designed for the harshest market conditions you can have, which is oil and gas, so we knew we could simplify them and put them into the industrial market where they don't need high pressures and where they don't have corrosive materials. We didn't know anything about that business, and it was like 25 years ago when we knew nothing about oil and gas. We rolled up our sleeves and got moving on it. Change is very important. A company has to be nimble enough to change and move."

I asked Scott about the laws of leadership he's developed over the years, and was certain he'd have a lot to say. Indeed he did. "No.1 is passion. It's the starting point of everything, for without passion, nothing else is achievable by any measurable value of success. No.2 is my team. I surround myself with exceptional people — people with passion, skill, drive, hunger and most of all, common sense. No.3 is persistence. Set your goals within reason and then don't stop pursuing them. Change, adapt, plan, adjust, take action. Whatever you do, keep moving toward your goal. No.4 is change. It's okay to change; recognize that and make it happen sooner rather than later. No.5 is procrastination. No decision is a bad one unless it's no decision at all. Stay in control of your future by deciding yourself where it's headed. Don't leave it to time and chance. No.6 is delegate. Once you have a great team, don't be scared to trust them. If you have gathered great people, they will make mistakes, but they will adjust and get great results. Always maintain control of your business, but do not micromanage. No.7 is relationships. Have good relationships with your staff and, most importantly, your clients. We pride ourselves on the fact that the majority of our clients have been with us from the beginning and I know most of them personally. I always say, 'Friends buy from friends.' Treat your clients as you would treat a friend, with respect and honesty, and they will stick by you through thick and thin," Scott finished.

I wondered which book had influenced Scott the most in the way he runs his business. He chose Ayn Rand's *Atlas Shrugged,* and was the second CEO to do so. "It's probably rather an unorthodox choice. I don't see it as a business manual per se, but I like the way it challenges traditional ideas and preconceptions of entrepreneurs. It promotes a pride in success and a passion in life and business. It's not directly related to business. I just wanted to read the book as I'd heard a lot about it. I read it probably 15 years ago. I didn't read it to figure out what I can do with CheckPoint; I really read it casually. And I liked how it challenged traditional ideas of business. I know that it's a very politically-oriented book, but I didn't read it as such. Instead, I looked at the characters and what they were doing with their businesses, and why." Scott said this influenced how he works within CheckPoint.

"Sometimes when you're working through problems, you doubt yourself. As a business owner, although you may be surrounded by many employees and even staff, you can feel very alone at the top. Reading that book made me think more about being a businessman, being an entrepreneur, what direction to head in, and what other people were recognizing. I have a quote above my desk from that book. It influenced me in a very positive way. Whenever I'm doubting myself or questioning some of the things I do, I go back and read some of my favorite pages and quotes and it makes me feel better," Scott said.

"When I read the preview of your book, I have to say that this is the exact type of book I wish I'd had at the time. While there are the *Seven Habits* books and others, those types of books never resonated with me. I would have liked a book like this one where I could feel like I was speaking or listening to people who have gone through the problems that I'm going through," Scott said. "I wanted a book that inspired me to take a leap to start a business, or to grow my own business. I feel that there's a lack of reference books out there. I would have loved to read your book 25 years ago," Scott said.

Considering his level of experience, I wondered if Scott had ever thought about writing his own book about business and sharing his success and experiences with others. "That's a good question. I still feel that the business is a work in progress, and it consumes so much of my time. We're going through a large transitional period right now, which has me back to my 18-hour days. At the end of all of this, I'd like to write a book. But I wonder if anyone would be interested. We're not Google, we're not Microsoft, we're not Facebook. How interested would people be in this story?" Scott asked.

I explained that there's definitely value to learning about the experience of a smaller company in comparison to the big juggernauts, which are relatively few. I shared with Scott that there are many smaller business owners who could benefit from hearing the experiences of businesses of a similar size. "That's a fair point. I read the history of Facebook, and Google, and Apple, but it's quite hard to identify my business with them," Scott said. "I've read a lot of books about Steve Jobs, and I love the way he controlled and made decisions that were short, sweet, and to the point."

To learn more about CheckPoint, readers are welcomed to visit www.cppumps.com. Scott said he does not spend much time on social media as his time is so heavily invested in the business, and his family. "I can talk to anyone, any time. If anyone wanted to reach out for advice or just for a conversation, or they recognize their own business in my business, I'd happily talk to people and meet them, and share it. I believe that entrepreneurs are the backbone of a country and its economy, so I love to encourage people to start their own businesses. It's a lot harder than people think it's going to be, but it's also a lot easier than people think it's going to be if you have the right mentor."

PART 4: ADAPTABILITY

When you are finished changing, you're finished.
-Benjamin Franklin

Adaptability can mean many different things to different business leaders, depending upon their area of expertise. But the most important thing to consider about adaptability is that a leader must keep his or her senses tuned to the business environment for signals of change. There are various traits adaptable companies share, such as acting on the signals of change, having the ability to experiment, managing experimental failure, retaining the ability to mobilize, and managing complex multi-company systems.

Many of us recall the early cell-phone days when most of the world carried little Nokia phones in their pockets. Nokia was an early mover and a known brand, but they could not compete once Apple came along. How did such a successful market-share leader flame out in a single decade? Easily, it seems. Apple utilized a small army of suppliers, partnerships and developers to create the iPhone. Apple managed multiple company systems, combining a vast array of talent to race right past Nokia. In fact, "smartphone" is now synonymous with iPhone.

But wait! Is Nokia really dead in the water? At its height in

2000, Nokia was the most valuable company in Europe. You might be surprised to know Nokia has a long history of reinvention with roots going back to 1865; to early beginnings in the forestry business. When Nokia was purchased by the Finnish Rubber Works 30 years later, they added a third business, Finnish Cable Works.

By the 1960s, Nokia had invested in electronics and telecommunications, eventually entering the mobile phone market in the 1980s. Nokia launched both the world's first handheld device and the world's first portable car phone. By 1998, as subsequent company iterations dropped all businesses outside telecommunications, Nokia became the largest cell phone maker in the world. Yet by 2007, Nokia controlled less than half of the cell phone market as Apple entered the picture and took over the market. By 2014, it seemed Nokia had no choice but to sell their mobile device business to Microsoft.

But Nokia just kept swimming. Now the second largest network telecommunications company in the industry, Nokia has once again answered their customers' call. It seems a new company is now marrying the Nokia-branded cell phones with the Android operating system.

I'm sure I don't have to tell you what a "Kodak moment" is, as the company's successful marketing and branding coined the phrase in redefining how we document intimacy. It is probably no surprise to learn that Kodak became the world's biggest producer for film, while its Japanese counterpart Fujifilm dominated only the Japanese market. How is it possible then that by 2012 Kodak would file for bankruptcy, while Fujifilm not only sustained their failing film business but reinvented the entire company?

It's all about execution. Kodak did not adapt to the blowing winds in the shift from film to digital. They failed to stay relevant when they did not shift production to keep up with a changing market, despite the fact that Kodak invented the first digital camera. They lacked the relevant expertise to manage the shifting tides. Fujifilm, on the other hand, began making new investments in technology and diversified into new businesses. As the film market deteriorated, Fujifilm dug down deep, and took a closer look at who they were and what they needed to do to adjust to a changed market. By investing in digital technologies, technical upskilling and other business diversifications, Fujifilm was able to stay relevant. Chances are you might be using one of their products when capturing your "Kodak moments" these days.

As I continued interviewing CEOs, it was clear that adaptability was one of the leadership skills that needed a separate chapter in this book.

Phil Wexler, The Fotoboyz

We adapt.

Unlike some of the CEOs I've interviewed who relied upon and perhaps required a strict and stringent vision, sometimes success requires that you be flexible. This has definitely been the case for Phil Wexler and his entertainment business. He credits his company's success to their ability to change. "Probably the biggest thing that we do right is to recognize that we're not afraid of anything. We're not afraid that Instagram's going to take over Facebook or that LinkedIn's going to take over print media or anything in any direction. I don't care what comes next. We watch trends and see what's hot and we have no problem with adapting. We adapt."

Talk about a fun business! Fotoboyz offers a wide range of entertainment options to "bring the fun" to holiday, personal and corporate events, including photobooths, casino and sports game rentals, a digital graffiti wall, and arts and crafts. They offer live entertainment, including magicians, steel bands, live artists, and even sumo wrestlers! With hot entertainment being a constantly moving target, I wondered how Phil and his crew were able to stay on top for so many years.

He answered, "We're never afraid of technology. We're never committed to one medium. We started out taking pictures using Polaroid cameras. I think within the space of three months we switched to video. This was before the Internet, so it was video the way you can imagine it was before there were digital cameras. There were no digital cameras. There were no cameras in phones. There was only film. The only thing that was faster than film was Polaroid. We had to be able to jump from that and never miss a beat."

Phil credits their ability to embrace new technology as a key factor to remaining in business for as long as they have. "In order to change and to look at technology as a blessing and not as an ending of our business, we see that it transforms the way memories are shared. You could say our ultimate vision is recognizing that we're in the memory business, not in the photography business. It's how you produce the image that makes it work. We're not even in the printing business, even though we print lots and lots of stuff. It's not important." He said that although they are in the photography business, they are not photographers and don't consider themselves photographers. "There are tons of photographers who are better than we are (or ever will claim to be) that are probably in the category of not being in business anymore. Or they're photographers on the side because they have to work a real job in order to sustain themselves."

I was intrigued by the idea of being in a "memory business". Despite all the technology and the phones with cameras and social media channels, at our very core we want to interact with others. We want to get out there and have a good time together and "act silly". Indeed, Phil's website has a tagline that reads, "We give you permission to be silly again."

Phil recounted a story about how being silly brought business to his clients. "Our team was at an event in Miami that was promoting tourism in the state of Florida. This was a conference being held by the governor of the state. He had to fight tooth and nail in order to keep the advertising budget to promote tourism. It's amazing to me that you would even have to think about the importance of that budget. He was told, 'People just automatically come to Florida.' No, they don't: they come to Florida because you've promoted that they are supposed to come to Florida. Of course, the weather's good and all that stuff but you still have to remind them to visit.

We worked a trade show booth for a client who was promoting their ecotourism website to all these vendors. After people participated in the whole long agenda, they needed something to break them out of the monotony of the whole process. We set up a photo booth in this client's trade show booth space. Of course, it was branded with their logo and information on it, but it turned out to be the best icebreaker ever, because all of a sudden, the trade show attendees were coming in there and acting a fool. I have a video of one of them asking the client, 'What is it you guys do anyway?' Then the salesperson from the company was able to say, 'What we do is we promote ecotours and we have this website that you can be a part of. You could be a vendor that's participating on the site.' The point is that we, providing the opportunity to have fun and be silly, were the icebreaker that got the conversation sparked," Phil explained.

Considering the constantly changing technology of the photography/memory business I was curious to know what was one of the biggest obstacles Phil's company had to overcome in these past 25 years. The answer made me realize that he truly meant what he said about not being afraid of technology changing. Naturally, I thought of Kodak and their inability to navigate those changing market waters.

Phil said, "It's very much tied to being aware that just because something was once very successful for you doesn't mean it always will be. There was the time when we had to go from an old DOS-based computer system, which was how we took the pictures, to a Photoshop-based system, in which we took pictures digitally instead of by video. My partner Michael was the one who took these printers (at the time they cost about $5,000 each and we must have had six or eight of them) and pitched them into a dumpster. I wanted to say, 'How could you do that? Oh my God!' But we had to do it. Despite the price, these old computers weren't even Windows-based, but DOS-based computers. We had to throw them into the dumpster, even though they still worked and you could still make money with them. But we had to do it in order to make the change to go to the next level. We had to be willing to throw out what was still currently making us money in order to change and go to the next level."

Phil's other challenge was to kill off a part of the business in order to remove the obstacle from their way. "Even if you have this money coming in, you may have to give it up to make a change. You have to give in order to get. For years we had a mobile-based business where we would go to huge events throughout the country — big festivals, big state fairs and such — and make items and take photos. It made a lot of money. By anybody's standards, we made a good living doing it. But the problem was our entertainment business was growing and needed more of our attention. We had to give up one existing business model that was making money. We did it slowly. Michael got out of it first. It took me probably more than 18 months when we were running both simultaneously before I was able to shut it down."

Phil said sometimes when moving forward you have to

know when it's time to "burn the boats." Killing off their mobile business left them with no choice but to move forward with their alternate source of income. "We knew we had to conquer. We had to make it work. We were ultimately successful with our venture and haven't looked back since. Once in a while, I would hear about this big event or that big event. Some were significant, definitely serious grosses of money. But I haven't looked back on it since we made the switch. Instead I wondered why I ever did that business in the first place, and wish I would have burned the boats earlier."

I usually ask CEOs about any laws of leadership they have developed in their 25-year careers, and how have they impacted their businesses. Phil admits he has never been well enough organized to have any laws.

"We don't take ourselves too seriously at all in the hierarchy of what we do. I guess one of the things I would say is that there's nothing I would ask anybody to do within our company that I would not do myself. Although a business can get to the point where you can't know everything, you have at least to be able to talk intelligently about a thing. For example, I'm not a Photoshop guy. I'm not an Illustrator guy, either. But I know enough that I can have a conversation with our graphic designers about the vision of how something's supposed to be."

Phil says his company never stops moving forward. "We were just talking this morning with our partner in New York about what we're buying. We were talking about what works and what we're doing here and what he's doing in the New York market and what's working and not working for us and going back and forth with what we need to buy. We never stop buying. We never stop spending money. It drives Michael crazy because he asks, 'Do you ever just make money?' I told him, 'No, we're never going to stop buying stuff. That doesn't work'."

They say if you love what you do you'll never work a day in your life. Phil exemplifies this saying. "Honestly, we love what we do. We don't just like it; it's something that we love doing. We love the whole experience of it, love everything about it. The only jobs I've ever had in my life were a bag boy in a grocery store, and in college I worked selling something from a vending company for about three months. That was it. I never worked. You congratulate me on 25 years in business, yet it feels like 25 minutes. We have so much more to do. We're not done growing, not even slightly. I tell our guys, 'You're not going to recognize this company in six months. We are never going to stand still.'"

Phil is inspired by Tony Robbins and has read many of his books and attended several of his events. "With him, it's kind of the same sort of deal: nothing ever stops. Each one stacks on top of the other. I just finished one of his books today on money. That book is probably not the most important one. It's very specific because it's all about money and that's not nearly as important as the reason that you'll get to the money if you have the right values. My favorite book of his is *Unleash the Power Within*."

Occasionally he considers writing a book of his own, but recognizes that penning a bestseller has little to do with luck. "That's not luck, that's effort. Lots of effort and time." Phil tells me some corny phrases he likes are, 'Luck comes to the prepared mind' and 'The harder I work, the luckier I get.'

To find out more about Phil and to learn how to act silly, visit www.fotoboyzphotobooth.com.

Adrian Velasquez, Fi-Med Management

Touch the magic of the moment before it passes by.

Since 1993, Fi-Med Management, Inc. has been working alongside healthcare providers and networks to maximize revenue and reduce risk — from catching billing errors to providing high-level safeguards against compliance risk. The company has grown exponentially over the last 24 years, becoming trusted experts in the fields of financial healthcare management, compliance and risk assessment, and chronic care management.

When speaking to CEO Adrian Velazquez, I wanted to know the No.1 factor that he attributes his success to.

"I would say creative problem solving," he replied. "The industry that we're in is healthcare, which is dynamically changing in rules and regulations with the new administration coming in. There's a lot of concern about what's going to happen with health insurance and how it's going to affect people. Healthcare is fraught with change and to meet that change, you have to be very creative and innovative in response. For the last 25 years, as things have been moving and changing, we've sought to be ahead of the curve.

Darwin understood that it's not the strong that survive, it's not the agile that survive, but it's those people who are able to change that survive. The environment changed so fast that dinosaurs couldn't adjust, and they became extinct. The same thing can happen with companies. You've got to adjust to the changing environment in business in order to survive," Adrian said.

I was curious to know what kind of changes Adrian had to make over the past 25 years to stay relevant in business.

"The first obstacle was 25 years ago, when I had an idea that I wanted to start a business," he said. "I was so excited. I thought the whole world couldn't wait for me to announce my new business. And then I announced it and nothing happened. All I heard was crickets, and it was so very disappointing. That first year in business I made zero money, and the second year I made perhaps $5,000. I became discouraged as I'd gone through all my savings already. I had a lot of questions, like 'Should I give up?' and 'What should I do next?' Then, all of a sudden, we got some traction on the east coast and on the west coast. And the business kept growing from there."

Adrian said, "The second obstacle we hit was a big one about seven years ago. At that time, we had our corporate office in Milwaukee, Wisconsin. We also had offices in Richmond, Virginia, Draper, Utah and Orange, California, with 127 employees throughout the United States. One of our large pathology labs had been with us for seven years and they were preparing for big national expansion, which would mean more growth for us.

Well, their funding didn't come through, and a company out of New Zealand acquired them. Six months later they pulled the business from us and we lost 50 percent of our revenue overnight. I was in San Francisco when I got the news and everything went black. I was absolutely devastated. How could I replace a customer that had been 50 percent of our revenue? Our biggest expense was personnel, so the immediate thing we had to do was close our Orange office. Then we closed our Draper office, laying off about 95 people. That was a horrible experience to bring 18 people in a room at a time and announce, 'Today is your last day.' Those people were very dedicated and committed, and I loved them all. But our whole infrastructure was set up for much larger cash flow, so it was an economic decision to lay them off." Looking back, Adrian admits to the extreme discomfort he felt. "It was a very fearful time because I was looking at the possibility that we might not survive, after I'd put my whole life's work into the business. If we didn't make it, what would I do next? Entrepreneurs don't like to work for other people."

Adrian's accountants, CPAs and attorneys urged him to file for bankruptcy. "That was not an option," he recalled, "I knew that instead I would grow the business. I would come up with a way to move forward. At the time we would meet almost daily to find out which bills we could pay. As our situation improved, these meetings were held weekly, then every two weeks, then monthly. And finally, we were able to make it through that time."

Adrian's story is a cautionary tale for entrepreneurs against positioning a client to provide 50 percent of the company's revenue. "Right before that time, I had a banker tell me he loved our financials. Together we went over our customer list, and we had about 40 at that time. The banker frowned and said, 'Adrian, you're in serious trouble here. One client accounts for half of your revenue.' At the time I was angry, but I later found out why he was right. It's very important to be diversified and that's why we now have three different divisions of Fi-Med. We no longer have one particular client accounting for a majority of our business," Adrian explained. "We learned a valuable lesson: it's important that you don't have so much tied in one customer, because they can hold that over you in negotiations. I would say one client should bring in no more than two to three percent of your business."

I wanted to know if Adrian's company was able to grow back to the size they were seven years ago. They're getting close.

"Last year was an excellent year for us, and this year will be another good year. Next year, based upon contracts and projections so far, will probably be the best year we've ever had," Adrian said. "We're not quite the size we were back then, as we're probably at about 50 employees now. But we're in the process of expanding our space by another 3,000 square feet, and we're hiring another 20 employees. We've got some major growth happening. We should be back at that point by next year. And in fact, even exceeding that the following year."

Adrian demonstrated his ability to handle what was a tremendous obstacle, but I wanted to backtrack a bit and learn how he was able to take his business from zero revenue that first year to where he is now.

"Creativity," he said. "Our company is located in the Midwest. Wisconsin is a very conservative state from a traditional values standpoint with a large German and Polish influence. It's very much a save-and-conserve mentality. I was new to the area, and I didn't know anybody or anything and was viewed as somewhat of an outsider. In other words, I had to find business elsewhere," Adrian explained. "I started working with people on the east coast, and there if it makes sense they just do it. The west coast is based on relationships. By going out of my area, I started getting traction on the two coasts to work with healthcare providers there. I had some ideas that I thought could work, so I tried them and they did work. We started growing fast on the east coast, and on the west coast. To this day, we have limited business in the Midwest, even after 25 years!"

I wanted to know if Adrian had developed any laws of leadership over the years.

"I have intangible laws. We have specific goals and objectives and look at how we're going to get there. Probably the biggest law is that I am responsible for the totality of the organization. When an employee succeeds, then I have succeeded. If an employee fails, then I have failed. Accountability means that anything good that happens is a result of my influence, and anything bad that happens is a result of my influence. I then look at the things I need to correct within myself to impact our employees," Adrian said.

He explained that his company promotes a very open environment where employees can say anything to Adrian. "I don't have to like it, but they have the freedom to communicate anything to me without fear of reprisal: good news and bad news. The other thing, as I mentioned earlier, is that any time I'm faced with something that's bigger than me and I can get overwhelmed, I am challenged to get bigger; to become more than the situation I'm faced with," he said. "During that period of major loss, I stayed focused on what I wanted to accomplish. I used adversity to assist me in focusing even more. I didn't avoid the adversity. I dealt with the adversity. Instead of succumbing to it, I used it to energize me while working toward renewed success. I'm a firm believer in intuition, and in trusting your hunch. That's how I move and operate."

I asked Adrian when operating from a place of intuition, how many times he will be right.

"I am correct 100 percent of the time," he responded. "I may have an expectation that it'll be one way and it ends up being another, but that brings me to a different place where I never would have been if I hadn't followed my intuition. I may create a sense of learning that I never would have had, or experience challenges that I never would have had. I place a high trust in my intuition and value it greatly. I believe it's something that everyone has, yet often over time they shut it off or deny it. Some people think the mind is more powerful. I don't believe that. I think intuition is more powerful."

While many CEOs have closets full of business leadership books, when I asked Adrian about his reading list he gave me an unusual response for a successful CEO.

He admits to not reading a lot. "I get bored. But I have a poem I love. Subjective writing is when you get into a meditative state and write words as they come to you. You don't pay any attention to what it is; you just write down your thoughts. Only when you're done, do you take a look to see what you've written. My wife wrote this poem and threw it away. I saw it in the trash, opened it, read it, loved it, and so I kept it," Adrian said. "It reads, 'Mystery of thoughts are magic tools to weave imaginary dreams. Seconds fly by and wondrous deeds are accomplished instantly. By night or day, it matters not what happens all about you. Success or failure is your choice of thought. Moments pass. Time keeps moving. What will be created next? Dreams enchanted. Love and hope are near at hand. Just touch the magic of the moment before it passes by.'

That last phrase is truly what I live my life by, which is to touch the magic of the moment before it passes by. It's like you're surfing and the wave comes. If you're too early, you can't catch the wave. If you're too late, you can't catch the wave. You have to catch it right at the moment, and when you do, it's an effortless ride on that wave. When I have a thought, an inkling, an inspiration, I don't have to know why. I pay attention to the sense that it's the moment, and there's magic in that moment, and I need to jump on that wave and ride it. That's how I live my life. It governs my decision-making process for the business, promoting and inspiring people within the organization. I want people to become greater than they ever thought they could be."

Adrian also enjoys inspiring others. "I have a client that just started a behavioral health business, and they're having some problems. They're trying to make it, but they don't have enough business yet. They lost three of their employees and it's been devastating," Adrian said. "I told her that I know how she feels. I shared that there have been times when I felt the same way. What I found was that with focus and perseverance, you can come through any test. I sent her a quote which reads, 'I asked for strength and God gave me difficulties to make me strong. I asked for wisdom and God gave me problems to solve. I asked for prosperity and God gave me brawn and brains to work. I asked for courage and God gave me dangers to overcome. I asked for patience and God placed me in situations where I was forced to wait. I asked for love and God gave me troubled people to help. I asked for favors and God gave me opportunities. I asked for everything so I could enjoy life. Instead, he gave me life so I could enjoy everything. I received nothing I wanted. I received everything I needed.'"

I can hear the passion when Adrian speaks. "I love doing what I'm doing. I find that every day it brings me lessons to learn, causes me to expand as a human being and create more of my life. My vehicle happens to be healthcare. We do revenue cycle management, which is billing for physicians' offices. We developed a predictive analytic tool internally to identify positions of risk of being audited by Medicare and Medicaid. We can also identify revenue potential. We're also doing something called a Well Living Initiative, which is assisting physicians in treating their patients, being a conduit of communication. We're national in scope, from Connecticut to California, and south to Florida. We have major hospital systems working with us. It's just a lot of fun because I love what I do."

You can learn more about Adrian and Fi-Med by visiting www.fimed.com.

Jeremy Enck, Fortus Group

Adaptability is the most important factor over time.

The Fortus Group, Inc. began in 1993 as the first specialty firm recruiting nephrology professionals for dialysis centers. In 2006, the company launched a travel nursing division attracting talented nurses with flexible benefit packages, competitive salaries, and focus on personal attention. In 2008, Fortus added an international division based in Germany. The expanding global economy and the heightened demand for qualified healthcare professionals worldwide influenced this decision. The division focuses on the direct placement of healthcare executives and clinical management, primarily in Europe and beyond. The company's international presence complements the success and industry expertise established within domestic operations, while creating a full-service solution for healthcare providers worldwide.

"Fortus Group does a couple of things very specific to healthcare staffing," Jeremy Enck explained. "On both sides of the world, we place people in direct permanent placement as well as long-term contract placement. We've got a small international presence. It's not a big part of what we do, but some of that does come up from time to time, as we're able to staff internationally as well."

I learned that *Inc.* magazine has named Fortus Healthcare Resources to the *Inc.* 5000, a list of America's fastest-growing private companies, for three consecutive years, so I was naturally curious to know what Jeremy considers to be his secret to success.

"The continued ability to be nimble, and the willingness to evolve in your given industries is the No.1 thing. Adaptability is the most important aspect over time," Jeremy said. "When the recession set in, I think a lot of companies were put to the test. They had to learn to be adaptable and lean during that period of time, like we did. We had to have leadership that was able to grin and bear it, and know that better times were coming, and not throw in the towel. Sustainability, or grit, is very important to get through tough times.

The recession forced us to get rid of some people that probably needed to go otherwise, but we figured out a way to continue to grow. We spun off another facet of Fortus Healthcare Resources into our contract division during that period of time, and managed to grow not just internally with our workforce, but externally with our contracts and the business that we conduct. I'm pretty proud of that. I think that said a lot about why we've been successful since the end of that recession nightmare. We've had a lot of growth and a lot of accolades because if you can grow during tough times and do it well, then when times are good, you can really succeed," Jeremy said.

The company's biggest obstacle thus far was to find a way to get through the recession period; to find a way to grow. "The only way we overcame that was to be adaptable. To overcome that challenge and get through it, we knew we needed to be more diversified within healthcare, and not so specific in just a couple of areas of healthcare. It's been a company initiative since 2010 to diversify and use our niche dominations strategy in business in multiple facets of different areas of healthcare."

It's clear the recession caused strife for Fortus. I asked Jeremy how his company was able to adapt. What did they draw on to inspire their team members to adapt?

"I'm praying that we don't see those struggles again," he said. "At that time, the founder of this organization, the executive chairman, Michael, would say, 'Keep the faith. We're going to grow through this period of time.' That helped me project that optimism to our salespeople; to help them stay strong and know that there was light at the end of this tunnel. His experience from previous tough times was critical for us to get through, because if leadership doesn't have the belief that everything's going to be okay, and we're going to get through this together, then obviously everybody else isn't going to be able to see it through either. I attest that to his experience, not mine, and it gave me the confidence to continue to lead through that period of time."

I asked Jeremy to tell me about some of the laws of leadership he has developed over his career, and how they have impacted business at Fortus Group.

"One of the most important things in leadership is to be consistent," he said. "There's a consistency in good leadership where you not only practice what you preach, but you walk the walk to show them the way. Consistency in your management style is very important. Also important is believability. A leader must be believable and respected. A leader also needs a high level of integrity. You do what you say you're going to do. It's funny but I don't know if there's a perfect answer to that question. I honestly just think you have to be an amazingly good person and surround yourself with equally good people. That's what creates a good leader: who you surround yourself with. Basically, your leadership is reflected by the qualities of those you have assembled around you."

I wondered which books have influenced Jeremy and the way that he conducts business the most.

"A funny one is by Paul Karasik, *The Sweet Persuasion*. It's an older book. It helped me succeed in business because it gave me hope. I think when people fail, it's because they don't believe in what they're doing. The book gives you a good way to walk into every situation, to feel confident in what you're trying to accomplish, and to put together a plan for being well prepared. Understanding the value of being prepared when going into any situation in business has really helped me," Jeremy said. "Also, *The Mastering Game* by Terry Johnson is a very good one. Lastly, and most importantly, is David Cummings's *Seven Habits of Successful Entrepreneurs*. Understanding the art of persuasion, and how to do it right so you can truly be a trusted advisor in any sales process or anything that you're doing — I think it's important.

Those books heavily influenced me as to what successful people do. Listen, I never felt I needed to reinvent the wheel. There was a lot of successful people before me. There's nothing wrong with replication. I read about how they set goals, and understood how they were unique in their process of either selling or whatever it is they were doing. Those books helped me," Jeremy said. "For example, if somebody said to me, 'Here's a wheel that rolls. It's a perfect circle,' and I need something that rolls perfectly, why would I try to recreate it?"

Jeremy has some advice for upcoming business owners. "Make sure you pick something that you can be passionate about and that you love to do. That's the No.1 thing. If you're passionate about what you do, you'll be 100 percent successful. Even when you're passionate and things get hard, it's frustrating. It can drive you crazy, but at the end of the day you like doing it. If you're not passionate about it and all those same things happen in that job anyway, then you don't want to do it. Otherwise, you'll always come back swinging like in a boxing match.

It's how I talk about business. Every round could be different. I might lose the first three rounds and win the next four. I have five things that I really attribute to being successful, and I'm hoping I can draw from them. I don't have the best memory in the world, but I can remember that if you're hard-working and positive, you're going to be successful if you're passionate about what you're doing, if you can do quality work, and if you can support company initiatives and management directions. You need the ability to not make the same mistakes over and over. You have to be able to learn from your failures, because failure is the foundation of success. But if you don't learn from failure, then it's the not the foundation of success. Then you're a failure," Jeremy said.

To learn more about the Fortus Group, you can visit www.fortusgroup.com.

Arun Gollapudi, Systech Solutions

It has been a constant reinvention.

Founded in 1993, Los Angeles-based Systech Solutions, Inc. has grown internationally with headquarters in the United States and India, and multiple service delivery locations around the world. Having completed more than 1,000 projects and forged partnerships with industry-leading technology providers, they have developed a full spectrum of data services, vetted, tested and refined to meet the specific demands and need of each company.

Systech has also established a global delivery center in Chennai, India, enabling on-site and off-site resources to work efficiently together for their clients' benefit. This allows them to bring specialized resources to a project, at the right time, wherever needed. Their commitment to providing clients with the most powerful solutions available has led to Systech's booming growth — being named one of the Fastest Growing Companies in America for two consecutive years by the magazine *Inc.*

I asked Arun Gollapudi, Systech's CEO, what he believes is

the No.1 factor for his company's success.

He said constantly adapting is the key. "We are always willing to look at everything we're doing, call what's wrong, call what's right and change as we need to change," he said. "Also, we have the willingness to admit failure; the willingness to admit that we were wrong and correct it. My partner and co-founder taught me humility and it became a constant thing. Every single year, it's been different at the company. We plan in December for what the year ahead would be like and make corrections. It has been a constant reinvention. We have a 25-year-old company, which is 25 different start-ups every year in the sense we examine and are willing to change anything that needs to be changed.

There's a concept of a flywheel in engineering which is this heavy thing that keeps rotating. All it needs is a whole bunch of small pushes as it spins because the momentum can be continued. Every little input gives it compound interest. It spins faster or keeps going for longer. That's the concept for our company. The company is running smoothly, but we find what tweaks are needed every year that make it spin faster or have more momentum," Arun said.

Every year they ask specific questions and they have come to recognize the kinds of answers that persist over the years. "We like the Hedgehog Concept from Jim Collins in his book *Good to Great*. We ask what lights our fire; what we are passionate about, what we are best at in this world, and how we can make money out of it. These guiding principles help us put that road map together for the coming year."

In hearing about Arun's questioning process, I wanted to know how he determined that data interpretation and analysis was his thing to go for.

"My partner and I came in from engineering computer science where we dealt with very large databases. That was a problem we were solving; our thesis, if you will. I started my

MBA program while working; in that program, I figured out quickly what the business is trying to get at in terms of answering questions by delving into data," Arun explained. "But they couldn't solve it 25 years ago because the very large databases were so big that only the biggest companies could afford to ask those questions of the data and get the answers. Even that would be very inefficient.

"When I worked for Nestlé, we would run a query at 8 in the morning and wait for the result to come back at 5 in the evening. It just ran through analysis for a whole lot of data. Today you get sub-minute responses for something like that. And that's a whole lot of design content that has gone in and evolved over time. But there's a whole lot of evolution in the computing space too. So we started off with very efficiently using all of the computer's resources for analysis of data, even in the very beginning, and to this day we do that. Today that data has exploded and the world has moved to our specialty. So in that sense, it's been a luck happenstance," Arun said. "We test our new processes and services in our own company before offering those to customers. In our own labs we instantiate everything we're trying out at times and most times we have already tested this out in our labs."

Arun said part of his success is being confident about solving the problem, suggesting the right solution, and if something is not working, to stay with the client until they have solved the problem, regardless of whether or not they made a profit. "14 years ago, there was a problem that we were solving at Walmart.com. The effort cost us something like 13 times what we charged the client. But we had to solve the problem, and after we solved, it we said, 'Thank you, here's the solution,' and told them we were walking away. They were very tough on us and said we didn't deliver the way they wanted us to. They made us redo the solution a couple of times over. And so we said, 'Here, we're done. Are you happy now?' They said 'Yes,' and then asked where we were going because they had the next project lined up for us.

"We told them we couldn't afford to do business with them because in this model we were the ones who paid for the whole solution and there was no partnering from them. They said, 'We understand'. In terms of the contract, we had to stick to it (our legal would have prevented us from doing anything different.) but said, 'We'll make sure we'll give you lots and lots of work, please come back.' Now this is our 14th year of operations at Walmart.com. They came through on that promise and kept us. After that, we've always been profitable with them. But that first project almost killed us."

I asked Arun if they tended to feel more confident about their services because they try them out in their labs first.

"We have either built it here or we have already proven it at another client because there's always variations about how something gets implemented at every client we go to. So in that sense, either we have checked out all the components individually or tested all the solutions that we deployed at a client and there's another piece that comes from another client. So we bring it all together for them. And we get them the references if they're doubting it, that sort of thing. Obviously, we can't hope to have had systems of the strength that Walmart.com or American Express or Nike have, but when we walked in there, we knew all the components that we took to them," Arun said.

Aside from the Walmart job, I wondered about other significant obstacles in Systech's development.

Arun picked an obstacle that most if not all of our CEOs had to surmount at some point in building their businesses: cash flow. "As a smaller organization without deep pockets, and without publicly raised funds, it was always a challenge. Thank God, but we haven't missed a single payroll in all 25 years — and it wasn't easy. There were times when cash flow was very tight. There were times when we plowed money back into the company, additional money on our own. But we never took a loan. We never raised public funds. We never needed other people's money.

But it was the best thing that could have happened. When things got tough, and when others might get things like margin calls, debt being called back, or certain stipulations from the bank, we didn't experience any of those things. We figured out how to work the whole process. We stuck to our core that we would not borrow money. We would not risk other people's money. And that paid off. I know others might say we didn't scale as we could have if we had borrowed money, but we could go to sleep easily at night. I know it sounds old-fashioned but that's who we were and it worked for us," Arun said.

Arun said once they started along that path, there was no turning back. "It was like we burnt the bridges that took us here. I came from a business family, one with many generations in business, but every one of them ultimately went down because of other's people money being called back or having to be repaid or things went south and they couldn't repay. So I've always been very adverse to raising money."

I asked Arun about his specific laws of leadership that impact his business.

He said that 25 years in the business, if it teaches you anything, will teach you humility. "We would have never expected certain things to happen, and then they would happen. Things would go wrong like you could never expect. Over the years we must have had more than 1,500 people go through our company. It was always about what kind of people to get on the bus — first, who to get on the bus and then after you get the right people on the bus, you have to figure out where to go and how to guide them and how to manage the team. How do you get the team all pulling in the same direction, or going along the same path? Getting the team on and guiding the team has been the biggest challenge and where we feel we learned the most. It's because we got the right people on the bus that we are succeeding today," Arun said. "Sometimes they come on for one purpose and they turn out to be excellent at something else. Once you know you got the right person on, let them figure it out or we'll talk with them where they belong and what they can do and how it can all play out for a common theme."

I asked Arun how they are able to determine if they have hired the right person. What do they look for?

"This could be a plus or a minus but what we always sought out was strength of character. Does somebody give up easily or do they never give up hope? We feel like the right person is the one who shows tenacity and the ability to hang in. The right person keeps trying different things and is flexible about it. The people who come in rigid may look very good on paper. They may have amazing qualifications but they don't belong in our team," Arun said. "So we look to see if they are passionate about what they do. Are they really good at what they do, and is it all a natural thing? It's about never giving up hope, and having tenacity."

Arun brings up James Stockdale, a U.S. Navy vice admiral and aviator who was awarded the Medal of Honor in the Vietnam War. "He was captured at the beginning of the Vietnam War and held in jail for the rest of the war, about seven years. They asked him at the end of the war how he was able to thrive when so many people who went in after him gave up and died. He said he relied upon hope. Those around him said, 'Tomorrow it'll happen. The day after tomorrow it'll turn. The American forces will be here in three months.' They kept thinking that while Stockdale only knew that he would get rescued. He just didn't have timelines in his head and he made every day work for him. He never gave up hope. I'm fortunate to have a gentle Stockdale in my partner. My co-founder is one such guy. He never gives up and I constantly learn from him. Stockdale's story is very nicely described in *Good to Great* by Jim Collins. That would be my all-time favorite book.

That book came out of the Stanford study where they took companies that were running along like the rest of the economy for 30-plus years. Suddenly, something changed and they started rocketing up and over the next 30 years they experienced dramatic growth. In the study they applied that criteria and looked through all companies over the last 150 or 100 years. In doing so they found a small handful of companies like that, maybe 11 of them, and they used the commonalities they found among them to bring out the concepts in the book. We saw the book halfway through our life, about 2002. We used it as inspiration. We read through it all and thought this is parallel to what we do, this is how we would react, but here's something we're not doing, and maybe we need to look at this. We, therefore, used *Good to Great* as a guiding force so it really happened. Three cheers to Jim and his team!" Arun said.

To learn more about Arun and Systech, you can find Arun on LinkedIn or visit www.systechusa.com.

David Susi, RSI Roofing & Solar

Seek out management coaching.

Since 1993, RSI Roofing & Solar has offered a range of roofing & solar services, from commercial to residential and everything in between. Located in San Diego, California, they are the chosen roofing contractor for re-roofing, repairs, maintenance, and solar for a variety of clients, from schools and retail to medical facilities and apartments.

Back in 1993, David Susi, owner and president of RSI Roofing & Solar, began his dream of operating his own roofing company. RSI is proud to be a member of several trade associations throughout San Diego County, including the San Diego Roofing Contractors Association, BOMA, IREM, SDCAA and CAI among others. Through these collaborations, RSI has been able to develop relationships within the property and community management industry and to network with other local businesses.

I was curious to know what David attributed his roofing company's success to.

"Willingness to seek help, to accept guidance and help

from others, and then to implement what I've learned from them at each juncture along the way," David replied. "I have always sought out management coaching. I got introduced to it accidentally about my third year in business. Once I started formal management coaching, my business doubled after the first year. I maintained some level of management coaching and coaching of my other employees and managers throughout our entire existence. I think that gives us a level of professionalism, a level of knowledge, and puts us on a different playing field from our competition.

It helped us establish a strong, well-communicated company culture to guide the behavior of all employees in all aspects of the business, from how we treat our customers to how we treat each other. It's almost like the constitution of our company, as in this is how we are going to perform," David said.

Given this is such great advice, I wondered how David chose the right business coach for his roofing company.

"I looked for a coach that was more in line with the size of my business at the time. Right now I'm with a group called Sage, but before that I was with Vistage. My first management coach was Ruben Estrada. He had a small company called Estrada Strategies. He specialized in small businesses," David explained.

"At the time when I was a $3 million company, if I was with Vistage or with Sage, I probably would have been too intimidated and unprepared for the conversations that are had in that setting. Being with the right-sized management coach or maybe one that's even specific to your industry is key," David said. "I know I'm in the roofing and solar business and there are a few coaches out there who specialize in roofing contractors. I think that would be a key ingredient to getting started on the right foot: being able to communicate with people who understand your industry, your business, and the challenges that you face on a day to day basis."

When I asked David about any particular obstacles his company faced along the way, he said quite humbly, "Wow. There are so many. Everything from hiring the right people, learning how to interview, firing the right people at the right time, learning financials, learning protective strategies such as accounting. I got embezzled. In 1997, I had only been in business about four or five years and I got embezzled. There's just an awful lot of pitfalls out there. Like I say, just having a management coach and a group of peers that you can discuss common issues with is just such a huge part of success. You're not out there trying to swim in the ocean alone."

I asked David if he would expand in general terms on how he knew something terrible like embezzlement was happening in his company. How did he handle that once he realized it was happening?

At the time they were still a small company. "I always had good credit. I would get phone calls from different vendors about being past due. The person that was in charge of things would tell me she sent them a check and she would show me the check. It turned out that she was using checks to cover money that she had stolen out of our Merrill Lynch investment account. It just took a while to surface. She wasn't turning in monthly accounting packages. I was too naïve to know that it should never go three months without seeing them. When it got to the third month, I had to demand to see the financials on my desk the following morning.

After that demand, she never showed up for work. That started the investigation. I hired an ex-FBI agent who located her. She ran out of town, left her husband, and went from San Diego to Flagstaff, Arizona. He was able to find her, get her to come back, surrender what money she had left. He put together the crime book for the police department so they could prosecute her, which they did successfully," David said.

His advice is to know your financials. "It's one of the key things that you need to learn early on. Know what you're looking for, learn how to protect yourself, have your banking statements sent to your house and not to your business. Have any checks sent to your house and not to your business when you're ordering checks for your company checking account. Maintain control and a log of every check that gets handed out to be printed. Be the only signer. There's a whole bunch of little rules about that sort of thing to protect yourself. None of which I knew at the time and that made me an ideal target.

The other challenge we faced was when I started my company, we were doing re-roofing and maintaining the roofs on commercial buildings. We worked with property management primarily. All I wanted was to serve my clients and they were all repeat clients. I worked with one property manager and they managed 40 or 50 different properties. For us, it was maintaining those relationships," David said.

"So when I started all I wanted to do was sell roofs to property managers. I was good at it. I started my business in 1993 with me and hired two guys. I had very little money — $7,000 total. I needed to use $3,500 of that $7,000 to buy a million-dollar general liability policy. The other $3,500 was my operating capital to start the company.

I had never done financials before. I learned everything, literally everything, from Day 1 either from someone else or by trial and error. I can tell you it's much easier learning from someone else. I would say learn what a business plan is and how to put one together. Learn financials and at least how to read a P&L and a balance sheet. Be funded enough so that you're not under-capitalized going into business. That's probably going to be the root cause of most failures," David said.

Another obstacle for David was sheer growth. "I've started several divisions in my company. We have five now. We started out just as a commercial re-roofing company. Then we started a roof maintenance division and we found a great deal of demand for that in helping people maintaining their roofing asset, which is a very expensive asset if you own a building. People don't realize it but roofs and parking lots are probably the most expensive things you have to deal with throughout the course of owning a building.

I developed that department as well. Then we opened a residential division. Then we opened a solar division. I can tell you the challenges with opening separate divisions are equal and the same as opening a brand-new company. The only difference is you have a structure already in place and you have a geographical location already in place and you have personnel and equipment already in place," David said.

Still in all, you have to get your message out that you exist and then you have to have processes and procedures in place to make that effort successful and profitable. Another thing that I didn't mention and probably another thing that new business owners don't realize is how important marketing is. I think marketing is almost the life blood of a company. If you don't have marketing that is creating opportunities for you, then how are you going to succeed if you don't have business coming in the door, or at least the opportunity for business coming in the door?

You've got to create that, you've got to have a plan for it, and you've got to have money to support the plan. Anybody who thinks that they can start a business without proper marketing is going to get a rude awakening. I know I did. I never understood how much commitment you had to have to marketing in order to be successful," David finished.

I asked David which laws of leadership or guiding principles he has developed over his career.

"I mentioned before that you need a strong company culture. You need to let people know what you're all about, what you're going to be all about moving forward, for your customers and for the community. Then you have to have a vision. I think one of the best vision statements I ever heard was Coca-Cola's back in the 1970s. Their vision was a Coke within arm's reach of every person on the planet," David said. "They communicated that vision globally, and that pretty much happened. My wife and I travel a lot internationally. You can go to the smallest village in the smallest country or the most remote area and still find a Coke. That's always stuck with me. Our vision is our tagline on all the marketing that we do, our vision is also our website, our vision is our email extension, and that is, 'When you think roofing, think RSI.'

ThinkRSI.com is our website. Think RSI is the extension of all our emails. Everything we do is Think RSI. You think roofing, Think RSI. We communicate that vision to every person in the company, no matter what level they're at or how new they are or how long they've been with the company. We want everyone as soon as they hear the word roof, we want them to think RSI," David said.

"Culture, vision and core values are the Top 3 guiding principles that you need to have well established and well communicated in your company so that everybody is on the same page, moving forward in the same direction. Then understanding — I hate to use the old-fashioned term of mission statement but understanding why we're doing what it is we're doing." David said.

"We're going to establish good practices in our industry, and we're doing it to grow a strong, vibrant company with a strong backbone. We're doing it to make profit so that we can improve everyone's life — everybody inside the company, everyone we do business with, our strategic partners, and our community. We give a lot of money and a lot of time to charities within our community and it's only possible by running a successful business and having enough money at the bottom line so that we can afford to participate in helping our community. To mentor each other and to hold each other accountable and all of the things that make a society work — we want to work in our small society, which is our company," David said.

It's no surprise RSI was nominated by the *San Diego Business Journal* as one of San Diego's "Best Places to Work"! I wondered which books influenced David the most.

"I read a lot of business books. As I look behind me here, I see a stack of probably 12 on my credenza that I've read. I pick a little piece here and there. I don't implement an entire book anywhere. Most of those revolve around education. We already talked about what the backbone of the company is and how it's set up and how you're expected to go to work every day," David said.

"There's only so much that I can bring to the table. I already told you that I started with pretty much nothing and had to learn everything myself along the way. I've also employed coaches and managers for my employees, for my sales staff, for my managers, so one-on-one coaching, peer advisory, is probably more effective for me in business and then passing that onto my employees through different types of coaching. As I said, I used Estrada, Action Coach, Vistage, and now I'm with Sage. I've afforded many of my people the opportunity to get coached as well," David said.

"I've used the *One Minute Manager* books by Ken Blanchard and Spencer Johnson. I like almost all the books by Peter Lencioni. He has been probably the one author that I've read the most. *Five Dysfunctions of a Team* was a good one. He had one out about the ideal team player, as I remember. Lencioni is probably the guru for business for any entrepreneur," David said.

David is understandably proud of the fact that he started

out with two employees and $7,000 and has grown to about 95 employees. They are on track to do about $14 million in revenue this year. To find out more about David and RSI, you can visit Google, LinkedIn and their website www.ThinkRSI.com. The website has many articles written by David.

Manoj Nigam, MicroD

Adapt and never give up.

In their early days, MicroD, Inc. pioneered the use of computers for desktop product presentations. As the Internet grew in popularity, their company took the technology and created the first online furniture presentation with ePreVue. Computer-generated visualization (or draping) kickstarted the next generation of innovation for the company and furniture industry.

Merging with B2B software company, Exim Technologies, in 2003, MicroD expanded the solutions they offer to manufacturers and retailers of the home furnishings industry to include electronic data interchange. Over the years, MicroD has patented the OmniVue® platform and was the first fully-integrated merchandising and marketing solution with product presentation, room planning, website development and hosting, and eCommerce capabilities.

I asked founder Manoj Nigam what he thinks are the reasons behind his company's success.

He said it's crucial to face your fears. "Don't avoid starting, or thinking, or executing on an idea for the fear of failure. If you believe in the idea, then try it. Don't give up. If there is a way around obstacles that you see, you will find it if you continue to believe in it. In the starting years of our company, there was a lot of competition around pricing and technology, but we adapted and we found a way. Then the ability to adapt and change with the expectations that the market place has kicked into play," Manoj said. "For example, MicroD has pivoted three times since I started the company. We are able to adapt and we're always making course corrections. So I would say adapting and never giving up were two of the reasons behind our continued success."

I asked Manoj how he advises leaders to face their fear, if they're afraid a business idea will fail.

"You work with all the data that you have in front of you and you make informed decisions and then you move forward with that and then try it out. Obviously, if you know for sure something won't work, then it's foolish to go there," Manoj explained. "Don't go by hearsay, or think that because it didn't work for someone else then it won't work for you. That is not a sure way. The No.1 way to fail at something is never to try it."

He acknowledges that in business you never have all the answers. "You go with what you believe in, with your intuition, and then if you have tried it out and it still doesn't work, then you find a way. But what happens typically is that when you go on that path, and maybe you come across a technology challenge that you can't overcome, you find another way to get to the same destination. I feel that once you have enough facts — not hearsay — there's a chance to try it out and believe in it, move forward and change."

I asked Manoj to describe one of the biggest obstacles his company has had to overcome in the past 25 years and how they were able to survive.

Manoj acknowledged there have been several obstacles. "The very first one I faced was we started as a company that had desktop software that we used to sell as a license. In the late 1990s and early 2000s, when the Internet became more of a reason to be with all of the dot-coms and everything that was going on, there was a push. The challenge we had was how would we — now that our software was no longer going to be on a per-fee / per-license basis — maintain our revenue if we go on the Internet.

Not only did we have to change technologically, we didn't even have skills in those particular technologies. We had to hire the resources and pivot completely to a new platform. We also had to figure out our business value population and continue to maintain the revenues that we had. So we hired a new team. I hired a new architect and did the entire transition from the desktop to online in about an 18-month period," Manoj explained.

I wondered if MicroD had always focused on the furnishings industry, or did they adapt later as business changed?

"I stumbled into the furniture industry through a dot-com that I was involved in. It started in furniture, and prior to that, I had worked in the automation industry. In other words, we build machinery which uses robots and other industrial technology things to build automation machinery. I'm a technologist, but found an application. But when I started, I would have partnered in one of the firms that actually did the machineries but when I started the company, it was actually in the furniture industries, home furnishings," Manoj said.

The transition for the technology and the business itself going from the desktop to the Internet was the obstacle Manoj faced. "We had to figure out new licensing models and work with customers on providing them. In fact, we actually did take a round of hits, but we expanded the number of customers, so we ended up at the same revenue levels or better, but we just had to continue to provide service to the customers in a way that they could hang on with us for the Internet product that we were building. It was key to hire people who could help make this transition and not be afraid to transform the company into a new thing."

I wondered what laws of leadership or guidelines Manoj developed in his 25-year career.

Manoj feels that leadership is a subjective definition. "Leadership is about inspiring people to want to do something bigger than they could by themselves. That includes me. I'm inspired by certain leaders who actually make our thinking bigger. You want to go and do something, and achieve a higher purpose than what you immediately could think of. Being with the right leader broadens your horizons. I have learned this from the people that I have considered to be my mentors. It's about inspiring people.

How you do that is giving people a purpose to be part of a group, or an organization. There's a number of ways to make a living, and you know whether you are a technology person or a business person, there are so many different avenues you can do that," Manoj said. "In my companies I have employees that have celebrated 20 years with the company. These are technology guys that have tons of jobs available to them, but they have stayed with us mainly because they believe in what we are doing, and they believe the company that we're working together in is not just the reason for making a living. It is because in a way we are transforming the industry and bringing something more than just writing a piece of software. That would be one of the lessons: giving them a purpose and a why of what our organization is, and then finding people who align with that purpose."

Manoj also feels that communication and integrity are

important. "You communicate what you want to do, but you must have integrity behind it. If you said you're going to do this, then do it. Do not make false promises that you don't keep. If you're transparent, then people will believe you in that if you didn't achieve something, they know you were very transparent in what happened and why we didn't make it there. So you make the course correction and go there, but integrity and people's trust in you is the key," he said.

"Another leadership lesson would be not to stop trying an idea because someone else tried and failed. Don't stop trying just because someone said it won't work. Also, never be satisfied with the status quo. In our company one of our core values is being innovative. We don't remain happy with the status quo, even if we may have the market leadership in a certain thing. You always have to innovate, Manoj said. "Innovation is not just in product; it could be marketing innovation. It could be the way we hire, the way our process works. New things that we are trying just in the office environment. Innovation is what keeps you motivated and forward-looking to be doing things.

Lastly, I would say — and this is on the personal level as well as at the business level — that I want everyone in our company to believe in a sense of full responsibility in a way that they have unlimited responsibility just as an owner does. They may have limited ability to take action, right? They can't act on everything. They don't have the authority to act on everything. But they do have the ability to respond," Manoj explained.

"If somebody sees something that's going wrong (even with me as CEO and there's something that they feel that I'm doing wrong), then they have a responsibility to come and tell me. I don't want them to feel that just because they don't have the authority to terminate something that they can't tell me. I may have reasons why we are doing it in that way, but I still want all the people in the company or even in the community to have a certain responsibility to suggest an action.

Responsibility in some ways could also mean respond-ability: being able to respond to what's going on around them. And who knows? They might think of something that I have not, and if they came to me I could take care of it," Manoj said. "I use a very simple example. An employee sees spilled coffee on the floor in the kitchen area of our company. Since it's not their responsibility, nobody can blame them for it. They're not accountable for it. But if they just walked by and did not clean it, they have failed in their limited responsibility. The responsibility belongs to either the janitor or the person who spilled the coffee, however they could respond to that event. They have the ability to take action and take care of it."

Manoj feels that as a founder and CEO, he is responsible for everything that goes on in the organization. "Respond-ability doesn't mean where to put the blame. Respond-ability means that I can respond to certain things. If I found that our product is doing something different from what we have promised to the customer, or it is not fulfilling what we had promised the customer, then it is our responsibility to bring it up, and let's fix it together.

The ability to inspire people for a purpose higher than themselves; the ability of a leader to communicate and maintain integrity; the ability to discern that it's worthwhile trying an idea even if someone else said it didn't work; the ability to adapt; and lastly, taking full responsibility for whatever happens around your environment," Manoj finished, "those are my guidelines."

I asked Manoj if there is anyone that he would like to mention by name that inspires his leadership style.

"Certain authors, such as Sadhguru, inspire me. He has

written books about inner engineering, and about how you should approach life. I have been inspired by him and his writings and his speeches," Manoj explained. "My very first boss was another inspiration that I felt gave me a reason to be an entrepreneur. I did not come from a business family, so I did not know how a business runs. But once I started my career, the first boss that I worked with had started a company and I saw that he worked hard and then reaped the benefits of it later. So I would say that might be somebody that I could say mentored me."

I asked Manoj which books have influenced him the most in the way he conducts business.

"The lessons that I regularly used in my business were from *Good to Great* by Jim Collins. Recently in our company we've been reading *Traction: get a grip on your business* by Gino Wickman. He's given a good script of what to do. Almost everything that he's talked about is something we do in the company. So he's given a blueprint, but the one thing that stuck with me that I really liked about the book is that 'less is more'," Manoj said.

Manoj learned you don't have to write 20 core values for your business. "You can write five but do them well. They should encapsulate what it is that you believe in as a company. I like this idea of 'less is more' maybe because of my engineering background. I like the brevity of things. The ability to express ideas with fewer words is what I liked about the book."

To learn more about Manoj and MicroD, you can visit LinkedIn or www.microdinc.com.

PART 5: CUSTOMER CENTEREDNESS

If there's one reason we have done better than any of our peers in the Internet space… it is because we have focused like a laser on customer experience, and that really does matter… in any business. It certainly matters online, where word of mouth is so very, very powerful.
-Jeff Bezos

You're familiar with the name Jeff Bezos, and you probably also know the founder and Chief Executive of Amazon has held the "richest man in the world" title a couple of times. Did you know however that he's projected to become the world's first trillionaire within the next 25 years? I'm sure you agree that something pretty incredible had to happen for Bezos to reach those peaks.

One of the primary reasons Bezos holds the first title and is in line for the second is due in large part to his well-known fanaticism about running a customer-centric corporation. Indeed the Amazon vision/mission statement includes a desire to be the world's most customer-centric company. They certainly hit their mark, as the Amazon brand has become nearly synonymous with over-the-top customer service.

As an example of his leadership, one story in particular bears repeating. To emphasize the importance of Amazon's most crucial and critical member of their company, Bezos is said to leave a chair empty in the board room as a reminder so that the executives always make decisions bearing the customer in mind.

Bezos doesn't stop at influencing the top tier of his establishment either. Two days per year, all employees — even the CEO — attend call-center training, and field live customer service calls. In this way Bezos helps his organization remain as customer centered as they've always been. It's difficult to lose touch with those who keep you in business if you're speaking directly with them on the phone, no matter your title or standing in the company.

"We've had three big ideas at Amazon that we've stuck with for 18 years, and they're the reason we're successful. Put the customer first. Invent. And be patient," Bezos says. He takes serving the customer even further — into the world of the future. It's not enough to perform for your existing customer base. You need to think beyond that first step. Warning businesses against becoming obsolete or irrelevant, Bezos urges them to be constantly figuring out ways to reach new customers to stay forever young and forever relevant. "I don't think you can invent on behalf of customers unless you're willing to think long-term, because a lot of invention doesn't work. If you're going to invent, it means you're going to experiment, and if you're going to experiment, you're going to fail, and if you're going to fail, you have to think long term." I'm inclined to take his advice to heart considering Amazon's standing across the planet.

Bezos is now competing against aerospace companies owned by Richard Branson and Elon Musk in what has been called "the billionaire space race throwdown". In 2000, he founded the aerospace company Blue Origin which aims to reuse their rockets to drive down the price of space travel. Blue Origin was the first private company to land a rocket, even before SpaceX. It seems that dominating the world wasn't enough for Bezos. In fact, he hopes his first space-tourism launch will take place in 2018! Mind blowing!

Back on Earth, in earlier chapters you met CEOs who recognized the importance of treating well both the people they hire and the people they serve on their road to success. Now we're going to drill down a bit in meeting a couple of CEOs who go above and beyond service.

Gus Avalos, Soccer and Rugby Imports

My determination to provide the best service to our customers is very important to me.

The Avalos family has been in the soccer and rugby business for 25 years. One of the interesting things I learned is they aren't in the business simply to sell gear. Their mission is "to work tirelessly to promote the game of soccer, as well as educate players, referees and their families about the sport and the proper equipment." Their passion goes beyond simply supplying customers with items. Like Jeff Bezos, the Avalos family thinks beyond the current customer needs. The mission statement of the family demonstrates this way of thinking: "We seek to provide the same quality of equipment as well as customer service to not only our local communities but to ALL. Our passion is deep and our objective is to spread it across America, and the world."

That's impressive!

Knowing that only one third of businesses make it past their tenth anniversary, I wanted to know what Gus felt was the main factor for their success. He said he considers himself a perfectionist. "My determination to provide the best service to our customers is very important to me. It's also crucial to have the right product mix and full shelves. That's key for our retail stores. Although we're a dot-com company, we also have five brick-and-mortar stores and that's where we do most of our business."

One of the most exciting things about this interview process is learning how these driven leaders leap over obstacles. In any business, you're going to have to learn to survive the challenges, right? Gus mentioned a challenge that considering the 25-year time frame we're working in, I'm sure many of our CEOs also had to face.

"One of the biggest obstacles we had to overcome was the shift to online buying. We had a webpage from Day 1, but more recently we've invested heavily to make it more modern and competitive with other webpages in our industry," he said. "We started selling online about 15 years ago and the online platform gave our customers more ways to buy. We still have screenshots from our first webpage, and it's definitely evolved a lot in the past 15 years. But about six years ago, we started investing heavily, and saw the shift of more people buying online. This has also expanded us from being a local store — a mom-and-pop shop in the local town — to more of a national, and even global, business."

Like all of our CEOs, Gus has naturally developed key leadership practices in his 25-year career. When I asked him how he feels they have impacted his business, he mentioned the importance of employee retention, and striking a key balance between admiration and respect.

"I like having my employees both respect and like me at the same time. Some of the things we do for our employees is to throw an annual holiday party, and buy them lunch every Saturday. Another thing we feel is important is to give our employees time off on days that most retail stores don't, like

Mother's Day, Father's Day, and Labor Day. While other retail stores are doing sales, we want our employees to be with their families just like the owners are. We are completely closed on those days," he said.

It may sound counterintuitive that Gus attributes their success to their customer focus, yet closes their shops several days a year on holidays. I wondered how his customers react to what may be unexpected and unusual closures.

"The next Monday after a holiday, we always get nasty emails and nasty voicemails," he said. "Customers ask, 'Why were you closed? You shouldn't be closed!' But I think on holidays they shouldn't be shopping!"

As always, I wanted to know which books resonated with this successful CEO.

Gus said he tends to read biographies or autobiographies on successful people. "I think the one that touched me the most was the Steve Jobs biography, because of how he was such a perfectionist and very detail-orientated. I didn't like how he sometimes treated his employees, but I did like the level of detail he went into. One example is how he would ship web orders to himself, maybe to fake addresses, just to see how orders arrived to customers. I've actually done that myself, just to make sure that my team is sending packages the way that I would expect them to. I've also read a lot of Richard Branson's books. I love his importance of having a fun work environment."

I honed in on Gus's mention of perfectionism. I know a lot of entrepreneurs tend toward having that trait. In fact, most entrepreneurs are said to have "perfectionitis", as I call it. I wondered if Gus felt that aspect of his nature has hindered him in any way, or if it has helped him in growing a business.

"I think it's helped me, but it also can mean working longer hours than I probably should, or coming in on a Sunday and Saturday. I'll work seven days a week if I feel the store is not where it should be. I could be focusing on restocking, or the layout of the stores, how product looks, or the way it's presented," he said. "There has to be a flow. The way the product is on the retail wall; it can't just be thrown up there with hope that people will buy it. For example, you can't have two red jerseys next to each other; you've got to throw a white in the middle."

Perfectionism can tend to slow down either a worker or a project. I wondered how Gus manages to balance perfectionism with flow.

Gus is good at multitasking. "One project could have been done faster if I didn't want it to be so perfect. I move onto something else, and then come back to finish that first one the way I wanted to. But it does slow things down, and sometimes it makes me work more than I want to."

Gus is the first CEO I interviewed who runs a successful, multi-generational business with multiple locations. They have four stores in Connecticut and one in New York that are run by eight family members: two sisters and their husbands, Gus and his wife, and his parents. "When meeting any of us, you'll get that family vibe. I believe it really shows that we all care about the business," he said.

Despite attaining success, I know it takes something special just to remain in business for a quarter of a century. I asked Gus what it is that inspires him to keep doing what he does. What is his motivation to keep going year after year?

"The biggest thing is the success that we're having. Year to year we keep growing, and with eight of us involved, I don't want to be the first to quit," he laughed.

You can visit www.soccerandrugby.com to read a brief background on the family and find out more about them. Or if you're in the neighborhood, visit any one of their retail store locations.

Mark Nureddine, Bull Outdoor Products

That driving force of taking care of the customer and making the customer No.1 is a solid focus to maintain.

It's certainly been interesting to meet the CEOs who head such a diverse variety of businesses. Take Mark Nureddine: he and his partner started the company that would become Bull Outdoor Products, Inc. out of their garage, when they created the deliverable "Outdoor Kitchen Concept". A year later the fledging company moved into its first location in what would be the first of many moves as they expanded operations to reach widespread prominence in the grilling industry across the world. The original outdoor kitchen concept has expanded to include a huge selection of outdoor kitchen works including grills, pizza ovens, carts, table, fire pits, and more.

Judging by the variety of their products, it's clear Mark and his team have learned to listen to their consumers and respond in kind. I asked Mark what he thinks is the primary reason he was able to take his garage shop operation and grow it into the type of success he's experiencing today.

"My answer might come up multiple times, because I think that it's very important for the sustainability of the business. My No.1 objective and priority has always been to take care of my customers. My decision-making process is to give customers a good experience with my product and my company," he said. "Of course, we have to make a profit. We have to have a sustainable company and product and operation, but it all derives from the idea that the customer and their experience with our company is the most important thing. Over time, this practice has enabled us to be successful. I started this company while I was really young, and when you're young like that, you can get sidetracked very easily if your focus isn't in the right place."

Mark went on to say, "To this day, we maintain that focus. It's important that I get that message to my people and that the people in the key positions in my company know and operate from the message that our business is all about the customer."

It's easy to look back at a business from the 25-year vantage point and see the progress of how it grew and survived over the years. Mark's website displays "The Bull Timeline: A Journey of Excellence" marking key growth and expansion points attained during the past 25 years. While the growth pattern looks so effortless, I wondered about the obstacles Mark faced as the company grew.

"Growth itself was the obstacle in our case," Mark said. "It's hard to grow, and I think the way we overcame that obstacle was by growing slowly. Our company is very dynamic in the sense that we have to develop product. We have to build that product. We have to sell that product. Then we have to service that product. So there are a lot of moving parts and a lot going on. You can grow, but if you grow fast, and you lose or do one of those things poorly, it can cause major problems in the company. You have to grow properly or you give yourself a lot of problems. I think growth is a big obstacle in a company like mine because of all the steps involved in getting our product to market, as well as keeping it there."

Aside from lasered customer focus, I wondered what Mark feels he's done right to bring his company to the level of success he now has.

"My philosophy is to surround myself with people much smarter than I and let them do their job. That's how I lead: I point my people in the direction that I feel we should go, and I like to let them take us there. I like to be the person who gives out the ideas and let the people who are experts in making those ideas come to fruition do their job. I'm not a micromanager as you can tell, and I think that helps us grow as a company; to do different things and do them well by letting the right people do the job they know how to do," he said.

I wondered how Bull's bottom line is affected by Mark's comfort in letting his experts take the wheel.

"I'm not a publicly-owned company, so I don't have to answer to anybody on our profits. Don't get me wrong, I like money, but it's not a driver for me. The driver is having a successful company, and in that definition, it's not all about the money. Sometimes having somebody come up with something that's a decision or a direction that isn't necessarily the most profitable direction — but is the right direction — is more important to me than just profit, profit, profit." Mark admits that may not be the answer for everybody, but it's the right answer for his company.

He was careful to cast his vision to his team to ensure that while enjoying the freedom to lead, they remain focused on the customer. "It's important to me, that as a company we develop and come out with new products, and we come out with new ways to deliver that product, and that we can do that from A to Z with the customer in mind. We're always thinking of the consumer. They're on our mind the whole way, throughout that whole process."

As always, I wondered which books inspired Mark's leadership philosophies.

"I'm not a big reader but I did enjoy *Built to Last: successful habits of visionary companies* by Jim Collins and Jerry Porras. That book stuck in my mind and influenced the way that I lead my company and grow it. You don't want the company to be solely relying on you. If I go away tomorrow, I want the company to keep going. I don't want the company to fail because I'm no longer here, if I'm no longer making decisions, if I'm no longer leading. I grow the company in a way that the people here in leadership can continue to run the company and move the company in the direction that I've built it."

Like Bezos, Mark is forward-thinking, considering the future of the company that he and his team have worked so hard to build. "That's a big deal to me, because I know I won't be around for long, and I do want what I do to continue. I don't want all the hard work — not only my hard work, but all the hard work from the people in this company that have grown it to where it is — to go away because I'm no longer here."

Mark mentioned a key point about the importance of finding guidance in books. "There's a lot of mistakes that young entrepreneurs make, and that I made, that can easily be avoided. I'd like to write a book because I feel that my story is important because I built a business without a mentor. I didn't have somebody like a father guiding me, because my father was not an entrepreneur. I now mentor my children. I help them. I tell them about all the things I did and the mistakes I've made. I explain how to do this and how to do that. But I had to learn all those lessons the hard way. I didn't have somebody on my side telling me what to do and when to do it and why to do it and why not to do it. If you can have that, it's great. If you don't, then reading books acting as mentors in helping you along the way would be a helpful tool as you build a company. I would love to tell my story, because I think there's a lot of people out there that don't have mentors and don't have that advantage."

I look forward to reading Mark's story soon, as not surprisingly, he has pushed forward with his goal to write that book he dreamed of. I was honored that Mark hired me to help him bring his story to others through my "done-for-you" book service. While you're waiting, you can learn more about all the grilling products and accessories Bull offers at www.bullbbq.com. If you're not hungry when you click, you will be soon!

Kevin Pludeman, Cornerstone Systems

We focus on the customer and their individual needs.

It's one thing for a CEO to develop a company and attain success, but quite another to build it in such a way that it survives ownership transfer intact. I was curious to see a successful example of this, and to learn why it worked.

Marshall Handelsman founded Cornerstone Systems, Inc. in 1993, with the goal to provide heat treating, finishing, galvanizing and coating job shops with an easy-to-use software program. His focus was on creating a program that was affordable and would help his customers manage their business activities more efficiently.

Marshall is now retired, and his son-in-law, Kevin Pludeman, has become president of what is now a family company.

"I'm very aware of the company history. I've been involved for a long time," Kevin explained. "The No.1 factor that I attribute to the success of the company is also what I feel separates us from other software companies in our market: that we focus on the customer and their individual needs.

Every company in our industry seems to have different ways of doing things. In our case, Marshall set up this company to be customizable and very flexible so that we can meet individual customer needs. That separates us from a lot of the other companies and allows us to have a good penetration in this market."

Sometimes a company's biggest obstacles are unforeseen, as in the case of Cornerstone Systems. Given that Kevin is so familiar with the company's history, I was curious to know what he felt had been their biggest obstacle to growth.

"In 2001, our main accountant didn't know if the company was going to make it. The country had gone into a recession, and we were still a young company at that time. While we opened the doors in 1993, we didn't have the software ready until about 1996, and that was when the regular sales really started coming in. By 1998, things were moving along at a good clip. We had a few years of ascending growth and then boom! 2001 came along and there were no more new sales. The company was burning through cash pretty quickly to meet all the expenses that year. Fortunately, by 2002, things picked up again, and the company survived. But there was a time when our accountant said she didn't know if Marshall was going to be able to continue too much longer. We were fortunate that the recession was short-lived," Kevin said.

I asked Kevin what he felt Marshall had passed down that enabled his company to survive a change in leadership.

Kevin felt it was Marshall's decisions to hand over the reins to his team during his tenure. "Marshall's primary focus was on the customers and trying to keep them happy. In doing so, he gave all the employees the freedom to do what they felt was the best way to do things. He definitely was not a micromanager. He gave everybody the flexibility to do what they needed to do. He treated everybody with a lot of respect, too. I never once heard the guy raise his voice to anybody.

That is his legacy that he left with the company," Kevin said. "The culture he created was to give people the freedom to come up with their own solutions to problems. Everybody has different strengths in the company, so everybody's allowed to contribute wherever they can. We all have positions in the company, but we can all contribute wherever needed."

I can see why learning how to be autonomous can give a company's employees the necessary tools to self-manage. It's obvious Kevin has given a lot of thought on how to continue Marshall's powerful legacy. I wondered which books influenced the way he conducts business.

"John Maxwell has written a few books that are very good. I've read some great leadership books, like John Maxwell's *The 21 Irrefutable Laws of Leadership*. Another one is *Good to Great* by Jim Collins. In that book he talks about certain companies that made the leap from being good to being great companies. From our standpoint, we are always trying to figure out what we can do to keep our company going, making sure we're learning about doing things that other successful companies are doing," Kevin said. "We've got a great group of people here, and that's one of the key points in *Good to Great*: hiring the right people. Our group here is very loyal to the company, and we enjoy an incredibly low turnover. Almost everybody we hire stays with the company until retirement. We are definitely trying to keep that going as we don't want high turnover."

Kevin made a point that I found incredibly interesting, as it was the first time a business leader had mentioned it. He explained they remain loyal to their employees and receive employee loyalty in return. "Today I hear many complain, 'Oh, people are not loyal to the companies anymore.' I think it's actually the other way: companies are no longer loyal to the people, so the people are not loyal back. We've continued to be loyal to everybody. In the whole time I've been with the company we have never laid anyone off. Not even during the recession of 2008-2009. We definitely give people the idea that they're very much valued here in the company."

Cornerstone Systems exhibits at all the industry trade shows, so if you are involved in their target markets, like metal finishing and heat treating industries, you'll see them there. In Chicago, Kevin serves on the local board of the metal finishing group. "We try to stay active in our markets, in the communities, and in the associations in our markets. Our website www.visualshop.com is the best place for getting company information," Kevin said.

Eileen Libutti, Lewis Johs Avallone Aviles

We aimed to treat our clients like they had a friend in the law.

Eileen left a big law firm with over 200 attorneys for a small boutique start-up. "I had two years under my belt when my senior partner Bill Lewis told me that he had left the firm with Fred Johs and Bob Avallone and he wanted me to join them. The initial goal was to be a small law firm that gave close and personalized attention to each individual that we dealt with. We aimed to treat our clients like they had a friend in the law. We strived to pay close attention to each client and each case, like you would care about a friend or a family member who was in need of an attorney. We wanted to make money of course, and be able to sustain ourselves, but in doing so, we didn't want to be that big attorney mill that just churned it out."

Unlike Shanin, who learned that their law firm's best tract was to "stay in their lane," Eileen and her team discovered the opposite was true for them. As a result of helping her clients with their diverse needs, their practice areas have grown over the 25 years. "We do a lot of defense work still.

Yet oftentimes an insurance company hires us to represent an insured person. That insured person could be a homeowner, or a driver, or physician. So not only have we had instances where the original claims person has an issue, requiring legal representation, we also develop relationships with these clients so that if they have another problem, they call us." Eileen said. This effort to give individualized attention to each client has made a big difference in their relationships. "We really connect with our clients. They reach out to us not only for that one case, but if they have other challenges, they will often call us and ask, 'Hey, you helped me with X. Can you help guide me with Y and Z?'"

Eileen explained that when you need a lawyer, you're often in a vulnerable position. She understands that lawyers have bad reputations. "Part of what we impart to our clients is that now that they have us, we will worry about the case so they can get back to their work. We develop trust. We'll speak to them when they need to worry, but they are free to go on with their day-to-day business while we take on the burden of the case. I will call and tell them when they need to prepare, and when there are things they need to be concerned about. I'm there to hold their hand and get them to their desired result. The best outcome is the one that meets our clients' needs."

On that note, Eileen shared a personal story. "During my first year in law school, a third-year law student was doing a mock trial. They asked first-year law students to volunteer by coming in to act as witnesses, so I agreed to do so. This law student was two years ahead of me in law school and said, 'Look, I'm going to hold your hand figuratively while you're up there. Don't answer questions right away. Take your time to think about the question, and give me an opportunity to object or intervene. I'm going to guide you through this.' They made me feel so cared for and protected that I thought to myself, 'I hope that someday when I'm a lawyer I can make my clients feel as taken care of and as protected as I feel right now'."

Taking care of clients can also mean watching how you spend their money. "A lot of law firms are looking to work the file. Sometimes the thought is if a phone call can fix the problem, send a letter. If a letter would fix the problem, make a motion. We always trained our attorneys to be economically aware," Eileen explained. "From the beginning our way of thinking was if we can solve a problem by picking up the phone, then pick up the phone. We try to do things in a very efficient way."

Eileen said it helped their firm grow by not only treating their clients well, but also their adversaries, and the employees of the courts. She said. "It's amazing how a little bit of kindness going forward comes back to you. It might not come back today, but you're paving the way for people to do good. As a young trial attorney, I would go into the Supreme Court in Nassau County and I would always greet the court officers, and after a while, those court officers became my friends, and sometimes clients. If I had to prepare in between my morning trial and the afternoon, they would give me a courtroom to sit in. They would bring me a sandwich if someone had lunch and send me a client or two along the way. It's all about treating people the way you would want to be treated."

Whereas Shanin found that his firm's biggest obstacle was overcoming bias against lawyers, Eileen ran into an obstacle she felt many similarly-situated firms would understand. "We started out doing a lot of medical malpractice defense work, and the clients changed their billing programs. The way that we were able to bill became much more regimented than before. You had to use certain computer programs. You needed to have certain stages of billing. There were things that initially seemed daunting. Being flexible, adapting to change, and being open-minded enough to see what our clients needed was very important in navigating those billing hurdles."

Eileen explained that the key to overcoming the changing landscape over time was to remain flexible and practice all kinds of law, which was the opposite conclusion Shanin and his firm came to. The Lewis Johs list of specialties reads like a one-stop shop, covering litigations/trials and appellate practice, and including everything from transportation law to medical malpractice and real estate. Considering the firm has grown from just four to over seventy attorneys, they must be doing something right. "We didn't put all our eggs in one basket. We've always felt that we should have a little bit of work from a lot of different people as opposed to one big client, because if things change — like that one big client decides to go in-house — we'd be out of work. So we aimed to grow slowly and meet the needs of our clients, even as they changed. We hired lawyers with different specialty areas as we grew organically. Being flexible, being able to change with the times is very important. For example, when our competitors would learn that a client was changing their billing program, they wouldn't be able to work with them anymore. We instead strived to meet our clients' needs by being creative in a changing economic climate."

When explaining the laws of leadership Eileen has developed in her 25-year career, she echoed a common directive I've heard from several of the CEOs I interviewed. "I learned as a young attorney never to ask someone to do something that you wouldn't be willing to do yourself. My senior partners would come in when there was a particular deadline, if something would happen at the last minute, and that meant that we were going to have to stay late. They would never ask us to do something that they weren't willing to roll up their sleeves and do alongside us," Eileen said. "Another piece of advice is never put yourself in a position where you are going to be worried about the ethical implications of what you're doing. If you are someone who acts with integrity and your people know that, they're never going to put themselves in a position that is going to be marginal either. I feel we should lead by example."

Returning to the importance of treating others well, Eileen said that everyone at the firm needs to be treated like they're valued. They all need to be treated individually. "You don't have to treat all of your people the same, because people have different strengths, talents and goals. Get to know the people that you work with. For example, my legal assistant wanted to go back to school. She thought that was going to be important for her, although it was going to have a drastic impact on the days and hours that she was going to be able to work. But on the other hand, she needed to work full-time because she needed her benefits. So we found ways so that she could work alternative hours, such as to come in early in the morning. She had this desire to go back to school, and I wanted to help her. Commit to developing your people in a way that lets them know they are appreciated."

I haven't quite heard it explained that way before, even though one theme that comes across frequently during my CEO interview process is "Care for your people, and they will take care of you." When you take care of your people, you gain their loyalty.

Eileen went on to say, "Some people will worry that if you let so-and-so leave at 4 every day then everyone's going to want to leave at 4 every day. But that's not been the case. People have different needs, and in an organization, those needs aren't necessarily going to be the same. So you can accommodate one person's needs and still accommodate someone else's needs, because usually their needs are going to be different. That person leaving early might be willing to come in on a weekend, or early in the morning instead. It's not like I interview people and ask, 'What do you need?' But when you develop caring relationships with people they know that I'm going to do my best to hear them out and to make the fairest, most mutually beneficial arrangement I can, because I do care about them. I've learned that 15 percent of people leave their job because they want more money. Most leave for so many reasons other than that. We retain good employees because we value the good work that they do."

Eileen feels that in running a company, compassion is key. "When I was graduating from law school, my mother wrote something in my yearbook: 'I hope people never mistake your kindness for weakness.' Compassion doesn't mean weakness. It means thinking about that other person's position and feeling concern for them. That doesn't make you weak. In fact, it may make you stronger. It's been found when studying different military situations and different sporting situations that it helps the strength of the team to be compassionate."

Considering Eileen's compassionate stance, I asked which book has influenced the way she conducts business the most.

She said, "I try to be a problem-solver and bring people together as much as possible. I try to be a resource for people. Even if people are calling me for restaurant advice, whether it be a client or another attorney, I do genuinely like to help people. But a book that really did impact me was *Who Moved My Cheese?* by Spencer Johnson. I read it so long ago, but it's about mice, Sniff and Scurry, and little people, Hem and Haw. It teaches how to stay ready for change, as change is inevitable. The book teaches of a positive and optimistic way to embrace challenges at work and in life."

I was curious to learn of an example of when Eileen challenged herself.

She said, "About seven or eight years ago, one of my senior partners called to tell me he met a new attorney who reminded him of me when I was newly practicing. She had this special education practice advocating for students with learning disabilities. He asked if I would be willing to take on this new practice area. As it turned out, the experience in New York was that there were students with learning disabilities who weren't getting the services they needed. In fact, we ended up taking care of some of our own employees' kids, working with their school districts to get appropriate services. It was something I'd never done before, although I'd tried medical malpractice cases defending doctors. That was very record specific, and I dealt with experts as I tried those cases. This was a completely new area of law for me.

But in working with this young attorney who knew the law but had little trial experience at the time, we started this whole new practice area for us in a field of law that I really was not very familiar with. Reading *Who Moved My Cheese?* inspired me to stretch out of my comfort zone, and it made me realize that you don't have to know it already, but you can learn it. One of the things I discovered, and this has also been a thread throughout my career, is that as a young attorney, you might not have the experience that your adversary has, but you can make up for that by being the most prepared. I recommend doing so much homework that even an adversary's experience won't be able to trump your knowledge of the particular case or the case law," Eileen said.

Eileen ends with another example of striving to grow in her personal life. "My kids go to a private school in Manhattan, and many of the moms have different schedules. So in an effort to be still able to socialize and be with these great moms that I'm fond of, even though I have little freedom with my schedule, I try to organize workouts with them instead of lunch. Maybe I'll try a new gym and text a bunch of the moms. 'Meet me at 8 a.m.' We get to bond through a workout which allows us to keep up with our daily work/home schedules. I'll try different gyms in the city, especially if there's something new that's opened up. I try to experience different things and not be afraid to do that, because I feel that's such a great way to connect with people."

For the eighth year in a row, Lewis Johs Avallone Aviles, LLP has been ranked as Tier 1 for 2018 *U.S. News & World Report*'s "Best Law Firm" for their Medical Malpractice Defense and Personal Injury Litigation Defense, as well as Tier 2 in New York City for Personal Injury Litigation Defense.

To learn more about this impressive firm, please visit www.lewisjohs.com.

Steven Pivnik, Binary Tree

It's customer satisfaction to the nth degree.

Steven Pivnik, of Binary Tree, Inc., says it all started in 1993 when a large bank down the street asked them to write a software application to migrate their email data. Two decades later, technology transformation is the company's core business. They've helped migrate more than 7,000 clients worldwide and 40 million users, including moving over 7 million people to Office 365 alone.

"If I had to pick one and only one thing to which I attribute our company's success — and I know this sounds very, very cliché — but it's customer satisfaction to the nth degree. We use the term maniacal around here," Steven says. "When I was an independent contractor, I was maniacally focused on making sure my customer was incredibly satisfied. I was first in, last out every single day for the duration of the project. And we created that culture as we scaled the company and brought on all the people that we have over the years across the world.

Customer satisfaction is in our DNA. The customer's

problem becomes our problem instantly. If I had a dollar for every all-nighter or all-weekender or all holiday weekend that we spent addressing customer issues, I'd have a lot more money. We enjoy the success that we have because of that approach to customer satisfaction. So if I had to pick one, only one, it's really that: do right by your customers and your business will grow and prosper," Steven said.

"For example, in 1993, we were a consulting organization doing really fancy custom application development for customers. One customer, J.P. Morgan, said, 'We have this project for you. We need you to write a program to convert email data.' My knee-jerk reaction was that we didn't want to do that, as it would be incredibly boring, as well as a tiny project. But because it was our customer with a requirement, we agreed to help them," Steven explained. "There was nobody available at the time in the company to do that project. Because I had a long commute — an hour and a half each way — I wrote the program on my laptop during my commute over a couple of weeks on the train.

Again, we just wanted to satisfy our customer. We didn't want to say no. It was a boring project, but we did it. And that mushroomed into an entire line of business and that's pretty much what we're known for right now. One of many things, actually, but at the core, it's helping customers convert email data from one platform to another," Steven said.

I asked Steven for some examples of what that extreme customer service might look like.

"We convert very sensitive data. The most sensitive data in any company is in individual mailboxes and calendars," Steven said. "Everybody's calendar is filled with sensitive corporate and private information. And they're very concerned about that data being perfect when they convert across email platforms; for instance, if they're going from an IBM platform to Microsoft Office 365. When those calendar entries need to get converted, they need to be converted perfectly. One example is we had a CEO with a dog grooming appointment on her calendar for the weekends. Because of some daylight-savings-time issue that occurred during that conversion weekend, the data was migrated off by one hour. And for anybody who understands how hard it is to get a good dog groomer, you cannot miss an appointment by 15 minutes because you'll never get that time slot again. So this CEO was irate that the company's email platform was being migrated by this vendor — us, Binary Tree — and data was not coming across correctly," Steven said. "That was just one example of 'It's all hands on deck. We're working through the weekend. We need to figure out why we're converting calendar data off by one hour in some instances.' We fixed the dog grooming appointment and it never happened again."

I wondered what obstacles Steven's company has had to overcome in his 25 years in business.

Steven explained that a recurring theme for them that they continually need to overcome is "shrinking addressable market." He said, "Let's take migration conversion. We migrate ourselves out of business because let's say there was a trend. In the 90's companies were moving from a whole bunch of different email systems over to IBM Lotus Notes. The more projects that we did, the less addressable market there was left for us. We needed to reinvent ourselves and come up with something else to do because we were migrating ourselves out of business.

Basically, we took the same exact approach, similar technology, and applied it to a different trend. So, fast forward to the 2002-2003 time frame, companies were now leaving the Lotus Notes platform and moving to Microsoft Exchange, because Microsoft was becoming an enterprise email system. It was a big risk for us at the time because we were a big partner of IBM, but we knew if we didn't do this for our customers, we were going to hurt our business and miss out on a very large technology trend. So we applied everything that we learned in the 1990s to move companies to the Lotus Notes platform, and we applied that to moving customers to the Microsoft platform. Basically, our obstacle is that the more successful we are, the less addressable market we have, so we have to continuously reinvent ourselves." Steven said.

He said the reinvention becomes necessary about every four to six years. "Because we've done it several times now, we know what to look out for and how to approach the 'reinvention of ourselves'. Now we don't react to it. We're much better at planning for it and already have the next big thing in development even before there's a huge demand for it."

Considering the data, I wondered if Steven is able to predict what the next big thing is going to be and where his customers might be looking to move their data next.

"I can't take all the credit for predicting the Office 365 craze, but we were one of the early adopters from a technology perspective to provide capabilities to move data to Office 365. We worked very closely with Microsoft," he explained. "Instead of pricing the projects like we normally do, we gave them discounts just so that we could be part of the early adopter program and help some of their early adopters move data to Office 365. Coca-Cola is one example, as they were one of the very early adopters of Office 365. We sacrificed profit margin on the project, just so that we could be the ones providing the technology for the data move. We learned from it, made our technology better and better, and now we are the standard for moving companies' data to Office 365."

I note that this way of handling their challenge actually makes Binary Tree an influencer as well as the provider of the service.

Steven agrees. "Migration is a daunting project, because it's very risky. There's a lot of downtime possibility. There's a lot of possibility of disruption to the business. Nobody can live without their mailbox. Nobody can live without their calendar working and checking each other's schedules. So we basically — via a ton of examples and success stories — show customers that they can trust us because we do this all day, every day and their project will be just fine.

Our success has to do with listening to customers and listening to the market and identifying trends. When you hear something once or twice, it's not a trend. If you hear it once or more a week, and then once a day from various customers, or you're starting to read stories about it, then those are signs that there is a trend happening. Then we start some R&D efforts to address that trend," Steven said.

I asked Steven if he worked primarily with big corporate clients, or also small businesses.

He said that Binary Tree's forte is in the large enterprises. "The who's who of the global 5,000 is on our customer list. But we don't say 'No' to business, so we work with a lot of small customers as well. We have a lot of 100-user or 200-employee companies on our customer roster. But where we add the most amount of value is really with the large accounts, with 25 to 50,000 employees and above."

I asked Steven which laws of leadership he had developed in his 25-year career and how those laws have impacted his business.

"Leading by example has always been a huge belief of mine. I've held every job that exists in the company. At this point, there's no way I can do any of those jobs as well as everybody else can, but I think they can relate to me because I did have their job at one point," Steven explained. "I developed code in the past. I was in sales in the past. I was in customer support in the past. I did client projects in the past. I was our entire accounting department in the past. So just having that experience of being down there in the trenches and going down when needed helps build comradery with employees and helps with retention. We're really proud that we have below-industry-standard employee turnover. A company whose management is willing and able to go down into the trenches with their team when needed, contributes to that.

I love to praise. Again, it's cliché, but praise publicly, reprimand privately. I've seen a ton of examples of managers who don't follow this philosophy. They don't last here. If somebody does a fantastic job, you want to make sure the world knows about it. The team definitely appreciates it. Everybody appreciates the recognition that's being given. On the flip side, people are human, there are mistakes that are made, I've made a ton of them myself. You definitely want to take those into a closed room, get down to the bottom of what happened, learn from it and move on. I've seen too many examples of those conversations being done in public and that never has a good outcome. That's not good for morale. It actually kills morale," Steven said.

The last law of leadership Steven has is to encourage all his managers to build a bond with everyone on their team.

"Everybody has something in common, even though you may have totally different hobbies or families. There's always some sort of commonality. Find what that is and build that bond with individuals and it goes a long way when you have to ask somebody to put in a weekend or put in extra hours. If you're doing it with them, by leading by example, and if you've got that common bond, it just makes the entire effort a lot less onerous.

We have 160 employees right now worldwide. Even though we have three offices, for the most part we're a virtual company. Most of the people don't report to an office. They work out of their homes. When we were smaller, we would have a company get together once a year, around the holidays," Steven said. "There was a ton of people around the bar usually. Now that we're a little bit bigger, those things tend to be quite pricey, so we do it once every other year, as far as an all-company event goes. We do have a whole bunch of smaller regional-type events that happen throughout the year. Like our Kendall Park, New Jersey office is all going bowling tomorrow night. It's going to be 30 or so people. We also have an office in Delaware, and there are constant outings planned. So there are pockets of team-building that go on throughout the year."

I asked Steven which books influenced him in the way that he conducts business.

He said he particularly likes *Great CEOs are Lazy* by Jim Schleckser. It's about how exceptional CEOs get more done in less time than everyone else. Techniques are covered for getting work done while still having the time to spend pursuing hobbies and spending quality time with friends and family.

Rather than spending a little time on a lot of things, the best CEOs spend most of their time eliminating the single biggest constraint to the growth of their business. They spend a lot of time diagnosing this constraint before taking action. Only when the identified constraint is removed or improved, do they move on to the next one.

"Another book which I read recently which I loved is *Lovability* by Brian de Haaff. He's the co-founder of a company called Aha!, which is a product management tool for development," Steven said. "The premise of the book is to take a look at the interactions that a client has with your company from the very, very beginning to the very, very end and making sure that the client always walks away with loving every single aspect and interaction that they have with your organization, from the people that they speak with, to the material they receive, to the product that they used, to the support that they get, to the follow up that they receive. If you nail those and create lovability, you're on your way to a scalable business.

I promote that all the time. When I have a fantastic customer experience, I put it on our internal blog and I showcase that as an example. I might say, 'I know you guys do this all day every day, but I just want to share the experience that I just had and that's why I will continue to buy Apple products, or I'll continue to use Airbnb.' I just love showcasing examples of fantastic customer experiences. At the same time, I love showcasing when I have horrible customer experiences and I tell my team why it was horrible and why I hope they, or we as a company, never do what I just experienced," Steven finished.

On a personal level, he keeps a little adventure blog. "I'm crazy about triathlons and mountain climbing and I like to document all of those experiences. Sleeps9.blogspot.com is my personal adventure blog and a lot of people find it interesting. For example, I got to the top of Kilimanjaro, which was over 19,000 feet above sea level. I attempted the summit of Mt. McKinley in Alaska, and we didn't make the summit because of really bad weather. We got stuck at 16,000 feet for nine days and ran out of food and had to go home. There was no danger at any point; we were just waiting for the weather to clear and we knew exactly how many days of food we had left. When the window expired, we said, "Okay, we're done. Gotta go home."

To find out more about Steven Pivnik, you can Google his name, to read previous interviews, or visit his LinkedIn profile for some additional links, or visit www.binarytree.com.

Rupesh Patel, Zenique Hotels

When it comes to our hotels, we take care of our people.

Zenique Hotels is a world-class hotel ownership and management company headquartered in Burlingame, California. Formerly known as Central Valley Hotels, the company was founded by Raman (Ray) Patel in 1993 when he developed his first hotel in Modesto, CA. After the development of four additional hotels and the acquisition of others, the company was later renamed Zenique Hotels in 2013 by Ray's son, Rupesh, the current President and Chief Operating Officer. Zenique is known for creating unique designs with top quality service (what they call, "the Zen of Service") at each of their properties, regardless of the brand each hotel is affiliated with. They have earned an impressive list of accolades throughout their existence and continue to be leaders in the hospitality industry.

When I asked Rupesh to what he attributes Zenique's success, he said it comes from very simple things. "It's hard work, dedication, and utilizing the resources that are around us. We never felt like we knew everything, or that we were the best at everything, so we constantly talked to our colleagues, friends, and family, about learning new things and new perspectives. We consistently built our network to get assistance for ourselves, and also to assist others. When it comes to our hotels, we take care of our people. When we think of people in relation to our core values, we include both our guests and our associates, the reason being without associates, we have no business, and without guests, we have no revenue. Focusing on the basics is a key to our success.

We're in the hospitality business, which is a people business. For someone who is not 'a people person', well, this industry is not for them. The hospitality business is about building relationships. It's about taking care of people, and being hospitable, and being able to understand each person's situation. Hotels are travelers' homes away from home; thus, we treat every guest as if they were a guest in our own home," Rupesh said.

"I grew up in this business, since my dad first developed the first hotel. It was not only my dad, but the majority of my family and friends that are in the hotel business, so I've been around it since I was a kid. Growing up, I didn't necessarily want to be in the business, seeing the hard work my dad put in, and the late nights. When I was young, it didn't seem like something I wanted to do, and then as I got older, and when I went to college, I figured I didn't necessarily want to take over the family business. I knew it would always be there." Rupesh wanted to venture out and do something on his own.

Rupesh continued, "When I was in college, I changed my major from business to public administration and city planning, the reason being my dad started the business and grew it; he never bought existing properties; it was all new build. I did the city planning portion of it so that I could understand the city's side of development, knowing that I could learn the private side from my dad once I got into the family business. Even after I graduated, I still had that feeling that I didn't want to do hotels. I knew I wanted to develop, but I wasn't sure I wanted to develop hotels.

I did residential real estate for a couple of years after graduating from college. When we finished up our Holiday Inn Express in Modesto, a new build in 2007, it was a time when residential real estate was starting to flatten out and drop, so I thought it was a good time for me to transition to the family business. I joined in 2007 full-time as a director of operations, but even then, I wasn't that motivated to be in the business," Rupesh confessed. "Then I realized that it was in my blood, I was actually good at it, and I understood it really well.

I became fully motivated around 2008-2009. It took me 12 to 24 months to dive into the business, and that's when the downturn hit, in 2009. That really brought out the grit and grind in me in order to survive the financial storm. I knew we needed to work very hard, and be completely hands on. That's when I began learning a lot of skills and diving into details of the business that most of my colleagues didn't really look into. I started to become invested in being a more professional operation. We maintained the status quo throughout the downturn as that wasn't a time of growth for our company. We didn't have the capital to go and purchase new sites at low prices. I wish, in hindsight, I did but we just didn't," Rupesh said.

"Then in 2011, we purchased a La Quinta Inn and Suites at San Jose Airport, where we did a gut job renovation, received the Renovation of the Year award for all La Quinta brands nationwide, and we ended up tripling the revenues for that property in just a few years," Rupesh explained. "This rapid growth catapulted me to think, 'Now I need to take this business to the next level, and build an internal management company so that I can focus on growth, and the day-to-day operation can be taken care of by a team that we will build.'

So we started to explore developing our management company in 2014, and we hired a consultant to help us go through the right steps. Again, that goes back to our value of not thinking we know everything, and hiring the right people. We hired a well-known consultant, Tarun Kapoor, and he helped us for about two years as we built the foundation for our management company. Now we're on our own; taking off our training wheels, as they say," Rupesh said.

"We've built a very strong management team that does allow me to focus on the growth, and use my brain at the higher level rather than the day-to-day operations. We're currently in an expanding phase, and we have a hotel in Dublin, an Aloft Hotel, under development. We have a Hyatt Place in Paso Robles that's under development, and we have a couple of other projects that are in the early stages of planning that we're working on as well. None of that would've been possible if we hadn't gone through the steps of building this management company using the systems of Tarun Kapoor. That's how we got approved to operate with Marriott and the Aloft brand, and that's how we got approved to operate the Hyatt brand through the structure that we have built," Rupesh explained. "Even with the structure that we have built, we internally developed a really strong culture amongst all of our properties with our six core values that we developed. It has taken time to build it and make it strong, but we're starting to see the fruits of the labor now."

I wondered if having grown up around the business, and then having had experience in different aspects of the business, Rupesh felt he had worked at all levels of his company.

Rupesh said his father let it be known at a very early stage that the family business wouldn't just naturally become his. "He said I had to earn it. He never wanted me to work for him, because of the whole father/son dynamic, where within the family accountability might be tough. So I actually worked the front desk at my uncle's hotels during the summer, and I learned a little bit of that aspect, and at my other uncle's hotel I even assisted them with housekeeping at times.

Once I got into the business, I got my hands dirty, and I never felt there was a job that I couldn't do, or that I shouldn't do. If I come to the hotel, even as Director of Operations, and I see a spill, I'm going to pick up a mop and clean it, not go find a housekeeper and ask them to clean it up. I'll get my hands dirty even today as President & COO. If I see it, I'm gonna take care of it. That's leading by example. I'm not going to expect anything — and none of my managers should expect anything out of their associates — if it's something that we are not willing to do ourselves," Rupesh said.

As Director of Operations, Rupesh worked with each individual department, like a general manager's liaison. "I worked with housekeeping on different strategies and processes, and at the front desk, and in sales and marketing. I did this for five of our hotels during that downturn when we couldn't afford a director of sales at each of our properties. I did sales and marketing, and revenue management for five hotels. You could say I got my hands dirty in all different departments, and all different levels of the hotel."

Rupesh continued, "As people say, 'When you've been there and done that, it makes it easier to teach others.' Being in those different positions, and understanding our people in those different positions, gives us a better idea of how we can train them, and how to understand different people. Not every person learns the same way, and we have to be able to develop training programs and have people that work for us that are training others to understand those different people. So we have training guides, and we have strict procedures for training, but we leave a little bit open in terms of how the end user learns.

One person may learn by reading. One person may learn hands-on. One person may learn by watching. In our training programs, we cover all those different types of learning so that we ensure that we're covering all the different types of people that are coming into our business. If we're not training our associates properly, then we cannot expect them to work at the level that we want them to," Rupesh said. "How we look at it is this: if there's an associate that's struggling, we first look at ourselves. Did we train them the right way? Did we train them thoroughly? Before we point the finger at them, and start giving them disciplinary action, our first step is always to coach. If coaching doesn't work, then we go to the next step of disciplinary action, but our first option is always to retrain, or see where we may have made a mistake in the training process."

When I asked Rupesh about the bigger obstacles his company has faced in the past 25 years, I wasn't surprised to hear that surviving the economic downturn was one of their big challenges. "But I can go further back than that. Even bigger was an obstacle my father overcame, and that was taking a chance with an all-in bet. Prior to starting the company in 1992, he had been a partner in other hotels, however he had a different vision than what his partners had, and so he sold his partnership with them, and instead studied for seven years. My family was living off the income from the sale of that partnership, and for seven years he dealt with a lot of scrutiny.

People said, 'He was not the brains of that partnership before, you know,' and 'He's not doing anything for seven years.' My father white-noised all that negativity out and continued to study. Then in 1992, when he started the process of his first new-build hotel, again he had a lot of scrutiny around the community. People then said, 'He's building a hotel in Modesto, California. What is he thinking?' and "That's a place that has nothing. It's in the middle of nowhere.' But my dad had the vision, and he made an all-in bet."

Rupesh's father invested not only all of the money that he had at the time, but all the money that the family had at the time. "And it was his first new-build project. We were fortunate to have a very good construction company which we still work with today. It's the only construction company that we use for any project, which is Huff Construction out of Modesto. That all-in bet my father made was something that would be very tough for anybody to do; to have that confidence to make it work, and working hard to make it work, all the while knowing that if it doesn't, you will have to start from scratch all over again.

My father created a well-thought-out plan and vision, and it was the biggest risk to date. Even though the financial risks we now take have larger numbers, back then, it was an all-in bet: it was a starting ground. Luckily, it worked out. Since then, he's instilled in me that no matter what happens, we can overcome an obstacle large or small. Knowing that he did start from scratch and went all-in and made it work, and because of the foundation he laid, I have gained the confidence to take on any project. That was probably the biggest obstacle for the company," Rupesh said.

Considering Ray Patel's purity of vision, and complete commitment and passion for building his business, I wondered what that looked like at ground level. To make it work, did they find investors, or utilize family members before hiring employees?

Rupesh explained that his father always had the larger

vision. "He envisioned multi-property ownership. He was one of the first within our group of friends and family to become a multi-property owner. He always knew that micromanaging was not going to allow him to grow, so he envisioned macromanagement, and he went on to build five properties before I joined the business. He always operated it like a management company. He never worked at the property himself. He was always the higher-level, strategic person of the company, the CEO.

My father hired the right people, trained the right people, and always had a full staff at each hotel. He would hire the right GMs. He would build the GMs, and then he would trust the GMs to do what they needed to do. When I was young, I saw a lot of people within our community that are at their hotels every day, and they're making it work. And while that's not the wrong way to do it, he just had a different vision. He hired the right people, and then left a lot of them to run the business the way he'd trained them.

My father would say, 'The hotel employees know they don't need to call me unless the hotel's on fire, and even then, they would call 9-1-1 first, and then call me.' Our properties back then were an hour and a half away from where we lived, so there's nothing he could really do in an emergency anyway. He empowered our employees to make the right decisions, and taught them to be able to make the right decisions. I never had to transition out of working the front desk, or housekeeping, because of the foundation that he built with the right people in our company," Rupesh said. "Since then, we've turned over everybody, but having that knowledge of trusting and empowering the people that work in your company, is something I have instilled in the way that I built the management company, because that's the only way you can grow your business."

Rupesh said they experienced some transitions when it

came to building a management company around transparency. "Early on, we weren't as transparent about our numbers with our staff, and we realized we were not empowering our associates and our general managers. We recognized that we needed to steer away from that, and allow them to run the business at full capacity. Since 2015, all of our managers have had full transparency in our financial reports, and they present their financial reports. We tell them, 'You are the Chief Operating Officer of your hotel. Yes, I am the President and Chief Operating Officer of Zenique, but you are the COO of your hotel.'

We found they embraced the idea of the hotel being their business, and that they needed to manage their numbers and their expenses as if it's their own property. We allowed everybody to understand that this isn't my hotel, or Zenique Hotels' hotel, or the investors' hotel, this is *our* hotel. I believe that's the way that mentality should be. I credit my dad and the vision that he had from an early stage of looking ahead. He's always been an early adopter. I was fortunate to have that mentality from an early age," Rupesh said.

Naturally, I asked Rupesh about his laws of leadership that he's developed and how they have impacted his business.

"I always say that you have to lead by example. Stay humble, and never expect anybody to do anything that you wouldn't be willing to do yourself. You have to trust your people. You hire the right people, and you allow them to help make the company better. Collaborate with them. Never feel like you're above anybody else," Rupesh said. "I don't know everything in the business. Our team is our great brainstorming asset, so we always empower everybody to bring ideas to the table. It doesn't necessarily mean it will be implemented, but we encourage them never to be afraid to bring up new ideas, because it might be something that we didn't think about, or see from a different perspective."

When building SOPs for the management company in all the different departments, Rupesh collaborated with the housekeeping team and front desk team, allowing them to have a hand in how these policies and procedures were going to work. "What we may think works might be different from what a front desk agent thinks and that might turn on a light bulb for us," Rupesh said. "No matter what your position is, it's always a team effort. While, of course, the respect of hierarchy is always going to be there, we never treat our employees like they have to do something because I say so because I'm the boss. We've never had that culture. We model the leadership qualities that we have and build our leaders to have those leadership qualities as well. That's what makes a strong culture of people getting along, and that's how people produce, and are productive at a high level."

Since Rupesh helps his leaders feel invested in the business by giving them the power to manage their hotel, I wondered if they did the hiring at the lower levels using that same kind of criteria.

We created a full hiring process, and so we have strict procedures for the interview process. Actually it starts all the way at the job posting. It's in a specific format, and then it goes to the screening of the application, and then it goes to hiring where we have a two-step hiring process. There's the hiring manager who will do the interview, and we have specific questions that they ask and score them on. The first interview is a skill-based interview, and then the second interview would be the supervisor's supervisor, or the hiring manager's manager. For example, as a front desk agent the guest service manager would do the first interview, which would be a skill-based interview. The second interview would be done by the general manager, which is a culture-based interview," Rupesh explained.

Rupesh's company uses specific culture-based questions

that future employees are asked and score on. "This ensures that we're hiring the right people, not just for skill, but for culture as well. Culture is very important when you're hiring people. Somebody may have all the skills in the world, but doesn't fit into our culture, and that can really disrupt the production and productivity of the rest of the team. We definitely instill in hiring at all levels that there has to be that culture interview, and whether it's a general manager interview, or a houseman interview, the culture-based questions are the same."

I asked Rupesh about any books that have influenced him in the way that he conducts his business.

"I've never really been a book person. I've always been more of an article and blog person. I'm constantly learning from other successful hoteliers, other real estate entrepreneurs, and business owners through personal networking, and also on LinkedIn. I follow a lot of different people and business leaders from different industries. I follow their blogs and their articles, and it gives me different perspectives; not just the hotel perspective, but the perspective of leading different companies of different sizes, through different stages of growth," Rupesh explained. "It allows me to learn from different areas, and piece together what leadership qualities I want to have, or what type of business I want to have. I pick and choose from different leaders, and different articles, and different journalists' perspectives and put those together. So I can't really say that a single book has influenced me. Instead I learn from a wide array of different people."

Being in the San Francisco Bay area, Rupesh follows a lot of the tech companies. "I'm fortunate to have a network where I know some venture capitalists and others that are in the tech industry from start-ups. It's really interesting to learn the different perspectives of how start-ups grow and how they grow from culture. I learned how Google started, and about the culture that they have and how they take care of people. We're also fortunate enough to have a large network of people, friends and family, and those that we have met at different conferences that have different-sized companies, that have grown companies, that have been at the same level I've been at. Learning from others and their experiences helps us learn from other people's mistakes, and learn the different perspectives." Rupesh values all the people in his network, friend circle, and family circle. "I in turn help others that are part of my network at either the same stage of growth as me, or at an earlier stage where we once were. I really like helping other people, since we are where we are because of other people that have helped me."

I wanted to know about particular blogs Rupesh might be able to recommend.

"How I started was, before I got into LinkedIn, I read newspaper articles, business journals, and hotel magazines, but then I started joining groups of hospitality professionals, or hospitality owners, hotel owners, different groups, even on Facebook. Nowadays there are so many different groups of hotel general managers and things like that. I follow all those different groups and see what people post, and I utilize those," Rupesh explained. "Then I follow those that are writing those articles, and see what types of information they're posting on their profile, see their perspectives, and a lot of communications just start happening in those groups from one post. I like to read what other people's perspectives are on what someone has posted, and that grows ideas. Sometimes even if it's not something that that person wrote in their post, that might create a light bulb in my own thought process. There are just tons of different groups on LinkedIn that you can follow and see what people post.

A lot of my friends have said I should start a blog, or be a consultant for other people. I thought about doing consulting, but I don't want to steer away from my focus of growing my own company. I always make it known to friends and colleagues that I'm always available for phone calls. If they have questions, I don't want them to be shy. I'm always open to giving my perspective, or sharing my experiences. For those who I don't know, I still have an open door. I am considering consulting other companies in more depth in the future, once my company's at a stage where I feel comfortable steering some of my time and energy into helping others," Rupesh said.

When he mentors others, Rupesh tells them never to be afraid to ask questions. "A lot of people think asking questions means you're exposing yourself to being not smart, or not knowing everything. Not asking questions is probably the dumbest thing to do. One thing about becoming a good leader is constantly asking questions of various people and never being afraid to ask any questions to people no matter who they are."

To learn more about Rupesh you can Google his name or Zenique to see various interviews and webinars, as well as LinkedIn or www.zeniquehotels.com.

Galen Quenzer, Boys & Girls Clubs of the Sequoias

Trust in the community has helped us be successful.

Planning for the first Boys & Girls Club in Tulare County began in 1991 when a group of Exeter community leaders met to discuss the recent and dramatic increase in graffiti. They soon concluded that young people in their community needed a positive place to spend free time after school. The group formed a dynamic partnership resulting in the birth of the Exeter Community Center concept. The City of Exeter pledged $20,000 to help develop the Community Center project and an additional $30,000 to the Center for program support. Later that year the City of Exeter provided a run-down former grocery store as the fledgling club's first permanent building.

In early 1992, a countywide open house was held to show the new downtown 12,000 sq.ft. Community Center site. Exeter Public Schools and several contractors began contributing in-kind support, resulting in over $100,000 in building renovation. The Exeter Community Center was soon incorporated as a non-profit organization with an affiliation with the United States Boxing Association. By April 1993, the center had begun a new affiliation with the Boys & Girls Clubs of America and Tulare County had its first Boys & Girls Club.

When learning about the early days of the Boys & Girls Club, I am reminded of the old saying, "It takes a village to raise a child." I asked executive director Galen Quenzer why he thinks the youth center was able to grow over 25 years to where it is today.

"I don't know how many people you talk to that run nonprofit organizations, but I think it's probably somewhat different from a for-profit organization. Our organization relies on the community to participate in what we're trying to do. Our board of directors plays a key role in that, and having good people on the board is critical for us. I would say looking back to the beginning of this organization that has been a key factor all along," Galen explained.

He said that ultimately their success is measured by how well kids do, and whether they are successful. "A lot of times you don't know that for a long time, and you may never know that. Another way to measure success is by how much people are willing to contribute to your organization; how much faith and trust people have in what you're doing, and whether they are willing to contribute monetarily to what you do, and of course that helps keep you in business. We have been successful in that way, especially in the last number of years. I think we've gained a reputation, and trust in the community that has helped us be successful.

I couldn't think of a business or organization that could be more rewarding, and those are the kind of people we attract to work for us. Those are the kind of people I get to work with, both the paid staff, and the volunteers, and the board members. It's a unique, neat group of people I get to work with. That's rewarding, and just knowing that you're making a difference with kids in your community. What could be better?" Galen asked.

When hearing about how instrumental the board leadership has been for the club, I wanted to know what kind of people tend to be on the board.

Galen naturally explained that they look for people who have an interest in helping the community, as well as an interest in helping kids. "Some nonprofits, at least the kind that rely on contributions from the community, where they go wrong is they only look for that kind of person. They may know how to work with kids, or how to improve the community, but they may not have the resources themselves, or connections to the resources that you need as an organization to be successful.

We have people on our board who are leaders in the community, own their own businesses, are financially successful, know other people who are successful, and I would say what is very important is that these people are trusted in the community. Trust is huge for us. Those are some of the main attributes I think we're looking for in board members," Galen explained.

I asked Galen to tell me about one of the biggest obstacles that the company has had to overcome in these 25 years, and how they were able to overcome that obstacle.

"Well, there were two Boys & Girls Club organizations in our county. It's a fairly rural community in California, and so having two Boys & Girls Club organizations felt odd to me. I pushed for a long time to merge these two organizations. We finally did that six years ago, and in the process, the executive director of the other organization was determined that he would continue as executive director, and I took an operations role in the organization," Galen said.

The merger didn't go well because the organization faced some dire financial problems after a year or two. "There was an issue of trust with the new leadership, and so I was asked after three years to become the executive director again. It was a matter of restoring the trust, and staying true to our mission, and having that at the forefront of everything that we did. It was important for our employees to see that as well as our investors and our donors. They wanted to make sure that they could trust us to do the best we could with the resources they gave us. We rebuilt that trust. It took a bit of time, but I think we've done that pretty well at this point."

I asked Galen how they were able to rebuild that trust. I know many leaders have likely faced similar situations where they had to prove themselves in some way.

"We spent a lot of time communicating, but also following through and doing just what we said we were going to do. Transparency was important, and we made sure the community could see what our motivations were. I know they might look at me and ask, 'What is your motivation for leading this organization? Are you in it for the job, or do you really have a sincere interest in your mission? And in what you're saying you want to achieve?' People look at that carefully. They want to know we are passionate about the cause.

Again we're in a rural area, and there's a particular culture here. It's kind of the Midwest of California," Galen explained. "I've lived in the Midwest, and it's a similar culture of people. It's important who you are, as well as your integrity as a person and as a leader. That's critical. People don't go for slick. People around here don't go for that, so you have to be down to earth, and you have to have that authenticity."

When I asked Galen about his leadership style, he said the term "laws of leadership" didn't hit him right. I was interested to hear how he would answer my question.

"I would say I have no laws. It's about relationships on every level. That's what makes a difference in the kids that we are serving: the relationships that the people who work in our Boys & Girls Clubs have with the kids, the relationships that the leadership in our organization has with the staff who are working with the kids. It's the relationships that take place between our leadership, and the community, and our donors," Galen said. "It's about authentic, sincere relationships, not phony relationships. It's gratitude for whatever people are able to do and provide. Part of what develops good relationships is being grateful to people."

Galen also feels transparency is important. "Just being totally honest. Not feeling like you ever need to hide anything. Again, that's at every level. Transparency is attractive to kids. They know when you're trying to hide something, and they are turned off by that. They're not going to want to participate in what we have to offer if they sense it. The community sees through it, too. We never hide anything that we're doing. It's a big part of who I am anyway. I feel that putting the needs of others in front of our own desires is important, and I'm looking for people to work in our organization that have that same desire in their lives. We need to put the needs of our kids and families, as well as those of our employees, in front of our own desires. It just comes down to having an altruistic drive.

I don't know that it's anything that I learned from a book, but faith has been reinforced throughout my life. It's my faith in God. I tend to see that a lot; that faith in other people in our organization," Galen said.

I asked Galen if he had a story to share about why he started the Boys & Girls Club.

It turns out that Galen's father still works part-time for Boys & Girls Clubs. "My father has a strong faith himself, and he went to seminary. Through a series of events, he ended up working for Boys & Girls Clubs. The plan was to go overseas and become a missionary, but he committed to working for one year. At that time, in the 1960s, it was a Boys Club, boys only. Girls could only come on Thursday nights to do crafts.

It became a family thing. I loved as a kid to go to the Boys Club, but I felt I was never going to work for Boys & Girls Clubs. I mean that was something my dad did. Not me," Galen said. "I'm in clinical psychology. I started out as a therapist, and through a series of events I found that I enjoyed working with people most in an active way. I took kids up to the mountains to do adventure-based therapy, and at some point, I said to myself, 'This is starting to look an awful lot like what I knew growing up in the Boys Club.' I took a job with Boys & Girls Clubs, and was invited to come as they started this new organization in the county I'm in now. Watching my dad, and him being a role model for me, and seeing through a lot of years how the organization impacted the lives of people made me a believer in this organization. That's how I ended up here."

Galen doesn't read a lot of leadership books. "I've read parts of some, but one that I have read through, and one that really does exemplify my ideas of leadership is an old book, *How to Win Friends and Influence People* by Dale Carnegie. I've just now looked in that book, and it was first published in 1936. It's old, and you can tell by reading it that some parts are dated, but the main principles were true then, and they're true now. It's about relationships and putting other people first, and the difference that makes. Again, in all levels. Being sincere, being authentic, admitting when you're wrong, caring about the welfare of others, being humble — it's all in that book," Galen said. "The title is a bit off-putting to me, because it sounds a little manipulative, but that's not the intention when you read the book. That's the one book I would point to." Galen tends to write more than he reads, and not surprisingly it's to help others. "I write here and there to inspire, or try to inspire our donors, and my board members. I write about experiences that I see in our clubs, that I see kids having, and how I think that's happening."

To learn more about Galen and the Boys & Girls Club of the Sequoias, please visit www.bgcsequoias.org.

Laurie Adams, Women for Women International

Our dedicated and passionate supporters are our strongest asset.

Laurie Adams is CEO of Women for Women International. She is an innovative leader, strategist, and gender rights advocate with more than 25 years of experience in international development and human rights across Asia, the Americas and Africa. Her professional history includes two decades of field experience in Africa, including managing Oxfam's country programs in three African regions. Also at Oxfam, she led the creation of an innovation partnership to support young feminists called Roots Lab. She joined Oxfam after eight years at ActionAid International leading efforts from the South Africa headquarters to measure impact, strengthen learning, and build accountability for more than 40 countries, including leading transformation projects in India, Brazil, Nepal and Uganda. She holds a Master's degree in Public Policy Management from the University of London, a Bachelor's degree in Political Science and Women's Rights from Dartmouth College, and completed the Advanced Management Program at Harvard Business School. Ms.

Adams has appeared on many outlets, including ABC, CBS, NBC and BBC.

Since 1993, Women for Women International (WfWI) has served more than 462,000 women survivors of war in Afghanistan, Bosnia and Herzegovina, the Democratic Republic of Congo, Kosovo, the Kurdistan Region of Iraq, Nigeria, Rwanda and South Sudan. With a long-term vision for sustainable change and development, WfWI works with the most marginalized and socially-excluded women so they have the skills, networks, and tools they need to rebuild their lives, communities, and nations. Through Women for Women International's comprehensive 12-month program, women learn about their rights and health, and gain key life, vocational, and business skills to access livelihoods and break free from trauma and poverty.

I asked Laurie what she thinks is the No.1 factor for WfWi's success.

"Our dedicated and passionate supporters are our strongest asset. Women for Women International's work is supported largely by individuals with big hearts who contribute either through our sponsorship program or in the form of donations. We've been able to attract more than 400 thousand donors and sponsors in more than 80 countries because we have a strong mission and have made real tangible impact in the lives of women survivors of war," she said.

"Our mission is to support the most marginalized women in conflict-affected countries to earn and save money, improve health and well-being, influence decisions in their home and community, and connect to networks for support. This mission resonates with a lot of people who see the growing conflict and atrocities against women around the world and wish they could do something. We empower our supporters by giving them the opportunity to bring change in the life of a woman through sponsorship. WfWI's sponsorship program is a truly unique experience."

In a world where we are surrounded by the constant noise of technology, WfWI has made it possible for their sponsors to go back to basics and create a truly human connection with another person. "When you sponsor a woman through WfWI, you not only learn about her name, location, and background, but also have the chance to exchange letters with her and know her progress throughout the program directly from themselves. For only $35 a month, anyone can sponsor a woman to go through our transformative program and create a sisterhood, a special bond that will change their life forever. I am myself a sponsor and I've gained so much from being one. It is not just sending money somewhere far away and being done with it. It gives you the chance to see the tangible impact you've made in the life of a real woman. It is incredibly fulfilling," Laurie said.

"Another reason for our incredible supporter base is that we've proven time and time again that our program works. Today, research from around the world has proven that when women are empowered, their communities and nations thrive. We have known this and invested in the empowerment of women for the past 25 years and we've seen incredible results. When women join our program, they have an income of $0.34 per day. Because of the skills they build through our program, their income increases to $1.07 per day when they graduate from our program," Laurie explained.

When women join WfWI, only 30 percent practice family planning, but by the time they graduate that number increases to 87 percent. "They are also more involved in financial decision-making from home. While when they enroll, 63 percent say they take part in financial decision-making, at graduation 91 percent do. In addition, when women join, 10 percent of them say they talked to others about women's rights. By graduation, that goes up to 89 percent. Women who participate in the program also receive a monthly stipend of $10 which they often save or use for the emergency needs of their families. Through the program, women also connect with other women forming business associations and cooperatives together. They also join savings groups so they can pool their money and power and save money together, take loans, and expand their businesses. Our work is comprehensive and transforms women's lives in sustainable ways. That is why organizations and individuals alike have supported our work and sustained us for nearly 25 years."

The obstacles WfWI faces are unlike the challenges most CEOs would face. When I asked Laurie to recount her biggest obstacle in developing her company, she said, "We work in countries and communities impacted by war or facing current conflicts. Working in difficult and insecure regions is never easy and one of our dilemmas as an organization is figuring out how we can make an impact without endangering the lives of the women and communities we serve and our local staff members.

In 2016, we were shocked to the core when one of the trainers for our Men's Engagement Program in Afghanistan was killed while advancing our life-changing work. His death was a tragic reminder about how dangerous — and how essential — it is to work for women's rights in conflict-affected countries," Laurie said.

To overcome some of these security threats, WfWI places a tremendous emphasis on working closely with local governments, and religious and community leaders and elders to gain their support for their work. "In addition, we immerse ourselves in the communities we work in so we are aware of the values and realities in their lives. This is why our country offices in all the countries we work in — Afghanistan,

Bosnia and Herzegovina, the Democratic Republic of Congo, Kosovo, the Kurdistan Region of Iraq, Nigeria, Rwanda and South Sudan — are run entirely by local staff. Our local colleagues are our lifeline. It is through their energy, enthusiasm and dedication that our work can be culturally sensitive and truly transformative. Their dedication and support and their collaboration with local communities is key to our survival in dangerous areas."

I asked Laurie which laws of leadership she has developed in her career and how they have impacted Women for Women International.

She said the most important advice she can give to anyone considering entering the human rights and development field is to remember and celebrate our common humanity. "Our field often runs into the risk of humanitarians thinking they have all the answers and they are there to serve the less advantaged. The relationship between those working in the field and those being served is often seen as one-sided, giving to the disadvantaged, but the reality is that we learn so much from having the opportunity and the privilege to serve others."

Laurie said that every day of working in that field is a lesson in human resilience, in how our similarities by far outnumber our differences. "It is our circumstances, not the content of our characters, that has led to some people facing more poverty, conflict, and violence than others. I try always to remember that I could've been one of the women we serve. Often our only difference is that I was born into a safe and loving home or in a region of the world that is not as volatile as others. We should work with people and communities in the developing world as equal partners because there is a lot that we can learn from those we are hoping to serve.

In fact, the lessons I've learned from global activists and leaders have been instrumental in my own professional development. I've learned the most on how to lead change from Women for Women International's Malian director for our DRC program. I've learned the most on how to campaign from my time in the pan-African movement. I've learned the most about strategy from activists and organizers in South Africa. There is a lot we can learn from our global counterparts that will make our work richer and more effective," Laurie said.

Naturally, I was curious to know which books have influenced Laurie and the way she leads the most.

"Even though I read on leadership voraciously, there is no one book I would point to as a major influencer. Rather, I have learned the most important leadership lessons from those around me," she explained. "One woman who comes to mind is Mama Lydia Kompe. She founded a federation of rural women in South Africa. Her organization was very successful and became well known, however she was not at all seduced by the power of money or fame. She stayed true to the vision of her organization remaining fully owned and led by rural women. She would turn down money and offers of help if it did not help strengthen that fundamental mission."

Laurie also learned a lot from Ramesh Singh, who lead ActionAid International when she was there. "His highest value was to remain humble. He listened very deeply to staff, and to all stakeholders, and did a brilliant job in leading change in the same direction — something I took for granted then but later learned just how challenging it can be.

Another leader who influenced me was my first manager at Oxfam, Jasmine Whitbread. She went on to lead the Save the Children Federation. Jasmine was excellent at remaining clear and focused in her feedback and coaching, in delegating everything operational so she could remain strategic, and in making tough decisions. I feel lucky to have had so many mentors, especially other women, who have taken the time to teach me valuable lessons in leadership, management, and activism," Laurie finished.

To learn more about Laurie and WfWI, please visit www.womenforwomen.org. You can also follow them on social media.

PART 6: RELATIONSHIPS

Great leadership is built on great relationships!
-John Maxwell

Leadership junkie, purpose weaver and catalyst Paul Sohn says five principles to be learned from John Maxwell are not only based upon relationships, but are the foundation for achievement. Rather than merely being the icing on the cake, they are the cake itself.

The Bedrock Principle maintains that a strong foundation built upon trust — beginning with yourself and expanding to others — will be more stable, secure and able to stand the test of time. The Situation Principle is about never letting the "situation" mean more than the relationship. In other words, let bygones be bygones. In the Bob Principle, problems are likened to fire starters. Since a problem can begin with Bob and spread throughout the company, it is imperative to deal with the first problem at once to prevent the spread.

Sohn references the old adage to THINK before speaking:

T – is it true?

H – is it helpful?

I – is it inspiring?

N – is it necessary?

K – is it kind?

Being at ease with ourselves, allows others to feel at ease with ourselves according to the Approachability Principle. Using a combination of warmth, appreciation for differences, consistency of mood, sensitivity and understanding toward others, the ability to forgive ourselves and others, and finally being authentic are key ways Sohn directs us to be approachable. Finally, the Foxhole Principle describes how having a friend who will fight with us in a foxhole, stand by us and believe in us is a key relationship to have.

Let's meet a few business leaders who stand by these principles.

Scott Joffe, Roufusport

I concentrate on having a healthy relationship with the people that I'm with every day.

Milwaukee, Wisconsin's Roufusport Mixed Martial Arts Academy is considered by many to be the country's top martial arts school for true beginners to serious competitors alike looking to learn kickboxing, boxing, jiu-jitsu, wrestling, grappling and MMA. They've trained world champions, such as UFC Welterweight World Champion Tyron "The Chosen One" Woodley and former UFC and WEC Lightweight World Champion Anthony "Showtime" Pettis. Scott Joffe's partner Duke Roufus is a four-time kickboxing world champion and one of the world's top striking coaches and MMA trainers. He is one of the most recognizable striking coaches in North America, and is considered to be one of the top trainers of Muay Thai outside of Thailand.

With such credibility in the uber-competitive MMA training world, I know some serious factors came into play for the academy to reach this pinnacle. I wondered what Scott personally felt was the No.1 reason for their success.

As John Maxwell said, great leadership is built on relationships. Scott agreed, "To pare it down to one factor, I concentrate on having a healthy relationship with the people that I'm with every day, that I'm doing business with, or talking to on the phone, or am living with. My two biggest reasons for success both have to do with marriage. The first is the support of my wife in my entrepreneurial endeavors. She's an intelligent woman and I value her opinion. When I first started working with my business partner in the martial arts industry, my background was marketing, advertising and public relations, not martial arts. My wife was the one who told me to stick with kickboxing, which was what we were originally doing years ago at our kickboxing gym. We had some professional and amateur kickboxing competitors competing on some of the biggest stages in the world. The support and advice of my wife was extremely important to the success of the business. Her mental backing and the support (not financial) that she provided and continues to provide is very important.

My other answer also has to do with marriage, and in particular my business partnership with Duke Roufus, who is a world-renowned, former four-time world heavyweight kickboxing champion," Scott continued. "Duke started his first gym in 1993 and next year will be 25 years for the school. We have 10 fighters in the UFC right now, and out of 340+ teams that have at least one fighter in the UFC, Roufusport is the #1 ranked MMA team in the world."

With such planetary dominance, I wondered how Scott defines a good marriage and a good partnership.

"In a good marriage, one of the things that you need to be able to do is compromise and look at things from both sides of the stick. I've always told my friends if your partner is not certifiably insane — and most of my friends are good, normal people and their spouses and partners are nice, normal people as well — then listen to what comes out of their mouths. My wife and I don't fight. We're going on almost 30 years together and this year will be our 21st wedding anniversary. We get along. We discuss things. We're a team. That's the way I've looked at my relationship with my business partner as well: we're a team. To achieve our goals and keep moving up the business success ladder, or the marriage success ladder, you have to stay focused on the big picture and not get caught up in the little things that most people end up turning into big things. They're really just little bits and pieces of minutiae that don't matter to the big picture."

Solid relationships equal solid success in Scott's world. "I enjoy my work. It's what I want to do. When business is going well, my relationship with my business partner is going well, and my relationship, first and foremost, with my wife is going well — I enjoy success. It's crucial to be able to compromise and look at things from other people's perspectives. Always keep the big-picture goal in mind. The relationship goals of a marriage are to be able to get along, not hold grudges, and put things behind you."

I remember learning in business school that you cannot have a successful business, or a successful career if you don't have harmony at home. When I share this with Scott he says, "Next to every great man there's a great woman. Sometimes people like the drama. They like to argue. I can't explain why people enjoy the drama of arguments and negativity. I think it's because they don't have enough big things going on in their life to occupy their time. While you're always going to be dealing with personal issues, you really should be dealing with things that are moving you forward versus things that are holding you back. You'll end up treading water when you have too much discord in your life. I've got too many big things going on and so everything has to be in harmony; I have to be in harmony. For example, I work from home. I stay glued to the computer and to the phone from at least, 8-5 every day. I've got an electronic drum set here in the house and I like to play that. But you won't see me jumping on this before 5. Even though I work from home, I'm working. I keep it peaceful. It's harmonious in all directions. My wife works for one of the Big 3 accounting firms so she's not home during the day. When she comes home, I realize that is her down time, so I have to adjust."

With such a positive attitude, I wondered what Scott's experienced as the biggest obstacles in growing the company.

"Cash flow was the major obstacle," he said. "I started my own sports marketing business in 1993 that booked sports celebrities for appearances and endorsements. It was a project-based business, so I only got paid when I booked a celebrity. It was sporadic: busy, then not busy. Luckily, my wife has been involved with the accounting firm that she works with for many years and the company she was with before that for many years. She's always had stability and income. But that didn't mean we had a lot of money. My business partner and I set goals and took on additional opportunities to make money in addition to running the martial arts school as it was getting going. We were definitely not living large in the beginning. We produced shows: live combat sports events such as kickboxing, mixed martial arts. We did those three or four times a year. Those shows would produce little spurts of income that would help us," Scott said.

The partners also found ways to cut corners. "Duke and his fiancée lived in one of the gyms years ago. One of the training rooms was their living room. It's just like when you hear about a guy who lived in his parents' basement while he started the business in their garage, or someone who lived in their music studio. Well, Duke lived in the gym and lived off of the earnings from his professional kickboxing fights."

Scott and his wife only bought their first home three years ago after saving for years. "We rented a small apartment in Milwaukee for over 20 years. I did odd jobs to supplement my income, such as painting, construction and demolition. If there was any other work to be had, I worked to make extra money."

The team remained devoted to their vision despite the challenges. "It was money in, money out, as we paid rent and utilities. We were in an old building and our utility bill was very high in the winter. The heat would leak out through the cracks in the brick. It was an expensive proposition to run a nice facility," Scott explained. "We knew that we had to scrape and scrounge and do what we needed to do. But we persevered. We wore many hats. Our staff at that time was very small, maybe three or four people. Now we're at 14 employees."

I wondered what attitude Scott had to take in order to get through those early days.

"We stayed upbeat. We stayed happy. We were patient. We knew our day would come if we worked hard. Now our day has come and we are the top-ranked MMA team in the world. One of our fighters is the UFC Welterweight World Champion. Another fighter, Anthony Pettis, was the UFC Lightweight World Champion. In 2015, he was on the cover of the Wheaties box for the full year — and we developed him from Day 1," Scott said.

I wondered how long it took for the team to overcome the "wearing many hats" period and become what they are today.

"It took us about 15 years to be able to hire the right staff to run the front desk and allow me to run the school from my home office," Scott said. "The gym is a very social place, so it's hard for me to get 'real work' done. It's supposed to be social. If students want to talk for a while, we'll talk for a while. Only within the last 10 years or so did we actually add on to our staff. We hired a second kickboxing instructor, a third kickboxing instructor, a Brazilian jiu-jitsu instructor, a couple of assistant jiu-jitsu instructors and the right people that could teach the kids' classes. Now we have people who are devoted, so the kids get to know their instructors and the adults get to know their instructors. It's not always a revolving door of people that they don't know."

Scott and Duke stayed focused during the early years as they were in the investment building stage of their business. "We didn't take the money in the beginning: we paid ourselves last. We still pay ourselves last. We stayed focused on the big picture. We knew one day we would get to the top of the mountain.

It wasn't so much about being No.1, but getting to the point where we could stay on top of our bills. That's always the thing when you're struggling in the beginning: staying on top of the bills. We knew we'd get to a point sooner or later that we would be able to pay everybody, pay ourselves, have a beautiful gym, have an excellent fight team and everyone would be happy with what they're doing. That's my long answer to what we did to overcome the challenge: we persevered," Scott said.

Now Scott and Duke's academy model has reached a level of success that other gyms seek to emulate. "We have a sense of community and an awesome environment at the school. We want to deliver an experience that people crave and can't get anywhere else. We consult with over 40 affiliate schools now, mostly in the U.S. and Canada, but also in Athens, Greece, and Melbourne, Australia, that want to learn how we do what we do. We give them their class plans and curriculum. Many of our affiliates emulate our environment, down to the look of our school, including our school colors, which are canary yellow and black."

I believe it's extremely inspirational to young entrepreneurs struggling in the first years of their businesses to read that it took Scott and Duke quite a long time to get to where they are. Now they're No.1, with affiliate schools and accomplished fighters. I wonder what advice Scott would share with these young entrepreneurs.

"The best advice I could give to younger people and new business owners is that it takes hard work and you don't know how much it's going to take. You have to wake up every day and be prepared to do hard work. There's no replacement for it; luck won't just come and do it for you. Luck is when preparation meets opportunity," Scott said. "You have to be prepared to work hard, to position yourself to capture those opportunities. If you're not prepared or positioning yourself to capture the opportunity, then luck doesn't even play a factor. When you get a job, it's because you trained for that type of work. You looked for that type of work. You put yourself out there for that type of work. You got that job because you did everything right. You weren't lucky; preparation met opportunity. It's hard work to be successful."

I asked if Scott had thought about specific laws of leadership that he developed, or by which he's led others by his example.

He urges people to learn to compromise and see things from others' perspectives. "If you're going to be in business with other people, then respect their opinions, respect their experience, respect their intelligence. Spread your passion for your business to your employees and others. I know you can hear it in my voice when you and I speak: I'm passionate about what I do. I love what I do. Spread that passion to your employees. Spread that passion to your customers. People will share it back with you. Our employees love to come to work at Roufusport.

Our staff never knows what UFC fighter is going to walk through the door next. They never know what awesome backstory a new student will have. They don't know what story a parent is going to tell them about the success their child is having since they started training at Roufusport. They're excited when an adult tells them they lost a ton of weight and feel healthier. Spread your passion for your business to your employees," Scott said.

Aside from casting vision and passion, Scott feels it's important to treat your staff in a firm but very fair fashion. "Praise in public, correct in private. They're adults. They are people just like you, so treat your staff the way you want to be treated."

Scott also recognizes the importance of cash bonuses. "Nothing says 'Thank you' more than cash. We don't give gift certificates to go get more coffee. We say, 'Hey, we had a great July. We won that world championship again. You guys are great. Next paycheck, you're going to see a bonus.' Especially with my front desk staff — they do a great job and are appreciated — we make sure that they get their bonuses. Share the wealth. Treat everyone equally."

I was very impressed by Scott's big vision. "Leadership is also leading the company. Diversify or die. Duke and I make sure to take care of business by creating multiple income sources so we can diversify. I definitely buy into the idea of being able to diversify: to turn on a dime, make a decision quickly, change with the times. Keep advancing, gathering information and intelligence as you're trying to go off in another direction related to the business. Always keep your risk factor low. Try to make decisions as quickly as possible. Assess your risk. Always base it on what's going to keep your risk the lowest. Don't let over-analysis cause paralysis."

Scott recognizes the importance of leading by example.

"We thank our employees often, virtually every day. We have a private Facebook page just for our staff. Duke and I track everything. Not only do we thank our front desk staff, who are responsible for keeping the school clean, for prospective student tours, for enrollment and for pro shop sales, but we'll also thank all of our instructors. 'Hey, great job on the sale! Thanks for creating a great experience that made this person enroll in Roufusport.'"

Like many, if not most, of the business leaders I interviewed, Scott believes in hiring the right people for the job, eliminating any need to micromanage them. "The hard work and the grind never end, so we make it fun for our staff. I don't keep them under a microscope. I let them do their job. They do look forward to coming to work but I'm not there overseeing them. They know I'm always checking the numbers. They know I'll walk in at any time and look for cobwebs. They'll know that they have to keep the gym looking spotless," he said. "Delegate responsibility and trust the people that you hired to do the job. Hire someone who's capable. But know you'll make bad decisions along the way. Then you'll have to make another decision quickly. Recognize a bad decision, and change or stop it right away. Nothing is ever cut and dry. It's okay if you change your mind, realize you made a bad decision or went off in a bad direction. Stop, assess what you need to do and go in a different direction."

By now, you've read this many times from our industry leaders, so you won't be surprised to read that Scott feels passion is important in leadership. "Your passion will spread to other people, I can't stress that enough. A good leader has to be passionate and other people will see your passion and they'll work just as hard as you because you're rewarding them as well. You're always praising. You're rewarding. You're criticizing only in private. You're treating them like human beings, like adults.

The kind of job people want to go to is where they're appreciated. We're only on this earth for 72 or 74 years on average. In that short amount of time, it's nice every now and then for people to feel that others appreciate them. Not everyone needs that. Some people don't care. They move to the wilderness and you never see them again. But for most people in work environments, a little appreciation goes a long way. A lot of appreciation says everything to an employee, or a staff member, that they need to know. Once they're appreciated, they will bend over backwards for that company. If they feel underappreciated, they won't. They won't do anything for that company beyond the basics. I heard someone the other day in business say, 'I'm just happy my employees give me a C+ effort.' That's what it's come down to? A C+ effort is now acceptable? I try to create an environment for everyone where they naturally want to give an A+ effort because they're part of the success. When our guys win world championships, there are bonuses that go out to the instructors and employees. We make sure that we share the wealth when we can," Scott said.

The book/movie that influenced Scott the most and how he lives his life is *The Secret*. "The law of attraction resonated with me; the idea of being able to create the world you want to live in. I truly believe that I envision the world around me. It causes me to keep surrounding myself with successful people; people who are happy, positive, optimistic, upbeat, nice and non-judgmental. If you hang out with losers, you're going to have a loser life. You're not going to be able to achieve what you want to achieve. If you hang out with winners, then you're going to have a winning life. It's just the way it is. There are no two ways around it.

What is that saying? You become like the sum total of the five people you hang out with the most. The law of attraction is something that's super important to me. Both Duke and myself had moments in our twenties where we realized there were certain friends that we had to depart from and not hang out with anymore. We wanted to move along in life. We both shed certain people in our lives. That was before I even knew about the book and the movie *The Secret*. It's just something I knew that had to be done.

I have the most beautiful wife that anyone could ever imagine having. She's sent from heaven. She is the sweetest. She is the nicest person. She always wanted a nice yard and a big kitchen. Well, she's got a huge brand-new kitchen now. She's got an acre and a quarter with over 800 trees. It's north of the city of Milwaukee, not way out in the wilderness either. We found a beautiful property, or the property found us, after looking at over 30 homes. My wife grew up by a pond, by a forest and now we live on Country Lane. How does that happen? How does this country girl end up living on a beautiful lot, in a beautiful house on Country Lane? How do I end up in the middle of all that? Because we create the world we live in," Scott said.

I find a lot of common ground with Scott and many of the other business leaders I interviewed. Even the most formal, who like keeping people at a distance, will admit that they believe in a form of the law of attraction, whether they name it this way, or not. Very often, they will.

To learn more, visit roufusport.com or you can look Scott up on IMDb.

Matt Frew, ShipZOOM

Have respect for everybody.

Although ShipZOOM was founded in 1993 as a product fulfillment center for the apparel industry, it has since expanded to distribute and service a wide variety of products. Their goal is to free their customers from all responsibilities associated with product fulfillment, and in particular, they place great emphasis on eCommerce fulfillment.

Matt Frew is the partner who adapts to all the different cloud-based systems of each company to ensure each order is processed, downloaded, and delivered to the customer's doorstep. He "makes ship happen" as they say. The importance of product delivery is the focus of ShipZOOM. "Every single entrepreneur out there who has created a product, well, this is their passion, this is their baby, this is their child, and we understand that and know we have to treat their children, essentially, their projects, as if they were our own," Matt said. In naming the No.1 reason for the company's success, Matt said, "We know that relationships are extremely important. We pride ourselves on not ever burning a bridge. Keeping good relationships is always important to us. Anybody who we work with knows that we treat them like family."

I know all companies face challenges, particularly when they've been in business for a quarter of a century. I wondered in particular how ShipZOOM navigated their challenges.

Matt explained, "The biggest obstacle we faced was when the recession hit. That killed a lot of businesses, which then affected us. We had to scale way back when we noticed that once the economy started tanking, people weren't purchasing any products. They were holding on to their money. If people weren't purchasing products online, we no longer had a business model. It was hard, but we had to let everybody go except me and my business partner. We were the only ones left in the warehouse. Only about three customers stuck with us through the recession. We're back up to about 58 customers and counting, and a larger staff of 15 people."

Navigating those tough economic waters will surely cause a company to develop certain ways of leadership to survive. I wondered what Matt and ShipZOOM learned and how it impacted their business.

"A lot of times we say, 'Treat others as you want to be treated', however I think it is really a concept of while you make sure that you treat others the way you want to be treated, definitely treat those people as if they're your own family. Essentially, have respect for everybody," Matt said.

Leaders are readers. I wonder what's on Matt's desk.

I see that the importance of Matt seeing clients as family carries through to his choice of reading material. Matt said the book that influenced him the most in the last 10 years was written by one of their clients, Russell Brunson. "*DotCom Secrets* by Russell Brunson has influenced our business a hundred fold. We do all of Russell Brunson's shipping and fulfillment so I've known Russell for over 10 years now. We've gone through the aches and pains of growing a business just like Russell has, with all the highs and lows. We've been right there with him. He's been by our side, and we've been by his side."

Matt explained, "One of our biggest lead generators is Russell and the Click Funnels team. Any time someone contacts Click Funnels and asks for help getting their physical product fulfilled, they are introduced to us. Again, it goes back to the relationship." Matt and ShipZOOM are perfect examples of how remaining loyal to customers and treating them like family pays off a hundred fold.

Although ShipZOOM has a simple website (www.shipzoom.com), most of their business growth occurs through word of mouth. "We've never paid for marketing. If anybody asks any of our other customers who they use for product fulfillment, they send them directly to us. It's all online. It's all word of mouth."

Steven Lowy, IKP Law

If you form a relationship with trust — which is our stock and trade — people trust you.

IKP is a full-service law firm specializing in civil litigation, entertainment, business, real estate, intellectual property, and tax and estate planning. The attorneys successfully argued a landmark First Amendment case before the United States Supreme Court. IKP's Steven Lowy has been practicing law for 40 years, representing a wide range of clients in the music, film, television, multimedia, fine art and related areas. His cases have included the estates of jazz legends, musical instrument manufacturers, independent record labels, award-winning artists, composers and producers in almost every musical genre, as well as numerous independent filmmakers, film producers, distributors, financiers, screenwriters, actors, personal managers, talent and literary agencies, software developers, motivational speakers, clothing designers, fine artists and an organic gourmet food manufacturer.

With such a successful career, I wondered what Steven considers to be the keys to success.

"I'm one of what are now only five partners. At one time, there were 10 or 11 of us, but many have gotten old or died and we haven't replaced them. One of the keys to success is finding very smart, highly competent and hopefully, well-adjusted colleagues to work with. That's the most sustainable aspect of the practice. All of my partners are very highly regarded in their fields and so when I have a client and they need help in other areas, the client can feel like they're very well looked after. Instead of having to refer them out to other firms, I'm there to oversee the other matter that may not be within my area of expertise. Since they have a relationship with me, the client trusts my judgment and likes me to keep an eye on things. It's worked out extremely well to provide my client an all-inclusive experience. You get a higher quality of client when you can offer a broader array of highly competent services," he said.

"When you're dealing with businesses, they don't just have music industry issues. They have employment law issues. They have tax law issues. They have corporate issues. Sometimes they get divorced. A lot of things can happen to people and if you form a relationship with trust — which is our stock and trade — people trust you." Steven said to maintain that you have to continue to deliver highly competent services and it helps grow the practice.

One of the biggest obstacles Steven faced was an unusual challenge for most CEOs: the death of the music business. "I've always worked for myself and I have a very general and broad experience in the law, other than the entertainment industry, as I keep my doors open over the years. I've tried a couple of dozen cases and I have a broad knowledge of the law and I didn't just limit myself to music industry clients, thank goodness. I have clients in other industries including film, television, fashion and dentists. I had a brother-in-law who's a dentist and he sent me dentists as clients for years and years and they're great clients. They pay their bills obsessively. They appreciate professional services. I had to learn a lot to be able to provide them the services they required, but I didn't mind."

Steven claimed this diversification was what allowed him to survive the ups and downs of the economy in general, and the music and entertainment industries in particular. "There was one point where I lost a lot of my film business and work because Canada offered tax shelter deals. That one year, with all these productions going up to Canada, I probably lost about $60,000 worth of work a year just to that one event. The music business has died. It's more of a hobby now. The profession has been put back to before Beethoven's time because he freed musicians from patronage. He changed that by publishing music and making people pay for music. Now once again people don't have to pay for music anymore. They can listen to free recorded music. Now musicians have to show up and play or they have to have a sponsor, which is no different than a Medici patron of some sort. I was president of the Association of Independent Music Publishers, so I've had to come up with these catchy little phrases. People still want, need and love music, but they don't feel they have to pay for it anymore. Now what you have is a whole generation that has grown up without having to pay. No longer are people dropping nickels in juke boxes all over the world while you're asleep. A musical artist's shelf life is typically very, very short. You're only cute for so long."

Not surprisingly, along the way, Steven has developed some laws of leadership that have impacted his business. "I'd say one, have patience. Two, try to look forward and not backward. Three, try to avoid blame and recrimination. Four, focus on solutions in the future. Five, stay positive and persevere. And six, empathize. These laws have served me well. I don't think everybody does business that way and different people have different ways of doing business that work for them. Some people like making everybody miserable and being a hard charger. That's kind of their brand and they can do well with that, but that's not the kind of life I chose for myself.

I found that a judicious temperament and a patient processing of information is usually a lot more effective than being reactive and vituperative," Steven explained. "I'm capable of fighting quite effectively. I've been a fencer my whole life and I've learned that movement is a premium; you only move if you have a purpose to move. If you're going to attack, you want to make sure you will be successful. Some people you attack, some people you don't; you defend. It's when you let your emotions govern your actions that it can lead to bad results. There are a lot of people who like to focus on recrimination, but that usually doesn't result in any positive outcome. If something bad happened, you have to understand the conditions that made that happen."

Steven said it's important to identify your weaknesses. "Everybody wants to concentrate on how great they are. Everybody's a legend in their own mind. But after you're on the planet for a certain length of time, you realize that there are certain things you're not very good at. There are certain weaknesses you may have. It might be an organizational ability. It may be a weakness in planning. It may be your memory. One of the important things I've learned how to do is to identify my own weaknesses and address ways of dealing with them. Sometimes it's as simple as just making myself do certain things at the end of the day to make sure I'm covered on certain things. Sometimes it's a matter of not taking certain types of cases or clients. Other times it's finding someone else to do something that I am not good at but they are. For example, I have partners who have different temperaments from me. One lawyer just may be a much better fit for a client, instead of my personality. It's not just about knowing how to identify and exploit your strengths. It's just as important to identify your weakness and devise strategies to safeguard yourself from yourself."

I wondered what inspired Steven to choose a career in law. His answer might forever change the way you look at law.

"When I was an undergraduate student, I studied mythology. I discovered that law is based on myth. Law is really based on narrative truth; it consists of stories that comprise the law. A lawyer's job is to tell their client's story in the context of all these other stories, which are the law, and to counsel them as to what stories they could live if they have choices to make. I realized in the study of Celtic philology that they would often look at the laws of a succeeding culture to reconstruct the mythic beliefs of a preceding culture. I thought that was very curious.

Researching it further, I realized that the law is not a science. Although people refer to all the arguments that go on in the law, you're really arguing about a story and its significance. The real edification and truth is in the actual description of events. That's how people order their lives in the law. In reading books that are well-written narratives, whether it's fiction or non-fiction, the telling of people's stories is what makes me most effective because it keeps the language accessible to me in the telling of stories in my own practice. As for books that influence me, they would not be business management books, but *The Cattle Raid of Cooley* (an ancient Irish poetic saga) or *Don Quixote* or Shakespeare. Books with well-used language, particularly in the telling of stories, are the ones that influence my practice the most on a daily basis," Steven said.

You can find out more about Steven at www.ikplaw.com and LinkedIn.

Lori DeVito, AET Environmental

We listen.

In *Relationships 101* Maxwell explains why listening skills can be a leader's best friend. It seems Lori DeVito, the co-founder of AET Environmental, Inc., was listening. This leader was recently recognized as a key influencer in metro Denver's energy sector by the *Denver Business Journal*'s Top Women in Energy program. Additionally, her company was honored as one of *ColoradoBiz's* Top 250 Private Companies.

AET Environmental was originally established to assist small manufacturers in disposing of their hazardous waste. This certified woman-owned business has since transitioned into a full-service environmental firm specializing in three areas of environmental services, including hazardous and industrial waste disposal, in-plant support and remediation and training and compliance. They support energy companies along with a lot of other manufacturing, and industry, and research labs.

They're now operating with a little under 30 employees, and Lori says they're on track to be close to $9 million this year.

Any business owner who has kept the reins long enough to celebrate a 25-year anniversary must have some leadership secrets. When I asked Lori what she attributes her success to, her answer was surprising.

"It was studying theater as an undergraduate in college," she said. "Theater teaches you to be aware of your surroundings and your set. Theater teaches you to connect with other people; to listen to what their needs are, so that you can create a response for them that satisfies those needs; that talks to them. For example, if a customer has a goal to be as green as possible, we listen and then put together a program that's going to give them as much recycling as possible. There's listening to what the words say, but also to what the person really means. Sometimes people will say something and the words are very literal, but you know that's not what they really mean. You have to dig further."

Lori shared that she learns from what others would see as mistakes. "I always tell people that a mistake isn't a mistake, as it teaches you that you need to make a different decision next time. If that didn't work, then move on. Don't beat yourself up over it. If you tried that once, and it didn't work, try something else."

I wondered what obstacles Lori faced as she built the business.

"There's a saying that I always use when we have something that needs to be done and everybody says they're busy. The saying is, 'If you really need something done, give it to the busiest person you know.' There are certain people who have a way of doing things so that they can work more in. They never say, 'No. I can't do that till next month.' I was one of those people," Lori said. "The biggest obstacle I had to overcome was learning to trust my team; not to do everything myself but to rely on the team. That meant I had to figure out how to hire people I could trust. It was a big challenge to stop doing everything myself and hand over tasks."

I asked Lori what benefits the company experienced when she started to let go of some of those tasks, and to trust others.

She learned that as she gave team members more responsibility, they took more responsibility. "They were happy to be contributing to the team, the community, the company, and to the clients they were helping. As you trust people more, and you give them more to do, they do more in return. They become the person that you can always go to. There's the debate between strategic versus tactical. Well, I was very tactical. Giving up tasks to those I learned to trust freed me up to be more strategic and think of longer-range plans for the company."

When I asked Lori about any laws of leadership she's developed in her 25-year career, she laughed.

She shared that someone once said to her, "'You're like Gandalf in *The Hobbit* because you never stop taking care of people or bettering this world.' I like the whole idea of deciding each and every day what I am going to do to make this work better. We have to decide what we're going to do with the time that's given to us, and fill that time with making sure we're moving towards the goal, whether the goal is increased sales, or that the project goes well, or being on track with our payables. Just be Gandalf, I say."

I wanted to know which book influenced Lori and the way she conducts business the most.

"*Blue Ocean Strategy* by W. Chan Kim and Renée Mauborgne. The authors put forth the argument that companies that succeed manage to create an uncontested market space, or "blue ocean," that doesn't have other competition in it. This is opposed to what they call "red oceans", where everyone fights about exactly the same product, with the metaphor being that red oceans are from the vicious competition turning the ocean red with blood and everybody dies. Blue Ocean Strategy talks about looking for something related to what you do, but that's completely different from what the competition is already doing. It gives you analytical frameworks and tools to figure out what that blue ocean could be for your particular industry," Lori said.

"This book helped me grow my company not just in telling project teams what to do, but in working with them to consider a problem or an issue from all sides, from outside the box. It's also helped us work on evaluating risks. Once that happens, it's easier for me to step back as a leader, because once we know what the risks are and we've evaluated things from all sides, then the team can find the best solution. I don't have to tell them what to do, I help them see things from a different point of view. That was one of the lessons of *Blue Ocean Strategy*." Lori uses the strategy for team development, in helping them to be more creative and think outside the box. "Once you've done that, every member of a team manages themselves. They have the freedom to arrange their schedules, arrange their work, take ownership of their project, their position, their responsibilities. The kind of company you get really depends on how every single member is fulfilling their responsibilities."

Lori also reads novels such as *All the Light We Cannot See* by Anthony Doerr, and a series of books that takes place in the city of Naples in Italy by Elena Ferrante. "All these books show complex relationships between people, and it's what I think about business; that things are more complex than simple, but it's important to stand back and see them from other people's viewpoints in order to decide what the proper viewpoint is."

I notice a trend surface amongst all these great leaders and their companies: they grow their people to take ownership of their positions. Team members learn to balance their responsibilities and their own lives. Lori mentions the importance of helping each other.

"We have to continue helping each other. For example, I thought I wanted to be a journalist at one point, so I went to the *Daily American*, a newspaper for English-speaking people. I was living in Rome, Italy and I was very young, like 22 or 23 years old. 'I want to be a journalist,' I said to the woman that ran it. 'I'll go anywhere in the city. I'll write about anything.'

She looked at me and she said, 'We don't need any more journalists. Go upstairs to the radio station.' I went up to the seventh floor, and sure enough, they were looking for disc jockeys to do their morning program from 6 to 10. A couple of days a week, I would do an afternoon program for children. It was really fun. It was back when we had the two turntables next to each other. They were LPs. I had to take the needle down on one song that I was playing. As that continued, I could do a little spiel in between, and then the next record was on the next one, and then I had to put it down on the right song that I wanted. This woman gave me the opportunity to learn that and to do it. I think we have to keep helping each other along in ways like this."

To learn more about AET, check out their blog on LinkedIn for their thoughts on environmental issues.

Marc Butler, Albridge

You need to know how to build the right relationships at the right time.

Although Marc points out that he has only been with Albridge Solutions, Inc. since 2010, he's well versed in the history of the firm. "The original business model for Albridge (formerly known as Statement One) changed significantly in the 1999 time frame. The company was founded 25 years ago, but it was a much different business then. There were several years when we didn't have any clients, so nobody knew who Albridge was until about 1999." Since then, Albridge has established itself as a leading provider of data management and financial technology solutions for broker-dealers and registered investment advisors. The company has created the award-winning Albridge Wealth Reporting™ solution which has received top honors in surveys conducted by leading publications, including *Financial Planning* and *InvestmentNews*. Recently, Albridge won an award for Outstanding Contribution in Wealth Reporting at the inaugural WealthManagement.com awards.

Marc attributes the company's success over time to hiring the right people. "Finding the right people is the key to our success. Whether in start-up mode or building the company for the long-term, we've been successful finding the right people and assembling a high-performing team".

I wanted to know the difference in the profile of these key players. Did Marc have specific best practices to share on how to acquire people that help run the company for the long-term versus people who help with a start-up?

"We have a great combination of people who were part of Albridge during its start-up years and people who have helped make the company more scalable as we've matured. We are successful because we remember where we came from, but are highly focused on the future. The key over time is seeding the company with talented people and developing the next generation of leaders," Marc shared. "As a leader, it's critical to put in place the next generation of talent and help them prepare to take the reins.

I think about building a team in Major League Baseball terms. You have a team that's in the majors, and then they'll have a triple-A team, a double-A team, and a single-A team. The farm team system, as it's commonly referred to, is getting players ready to be able to join the Major League team at some point. Not all of them will get to the Majors, but you want to seed the farm teams with people that will develop and be prepared to take the next step when the opportunity presents itself," Marc explained.

I wondered about the characteristics that Marc looks for in leaders or future leaders. Does he have a scorecard or a checklist he uses when he's going through CVs or inviting people to interview?

"A lot depends on the role, as we have a lot of different kinds of roles here. We're a fintech (financial technology) company, so we have some roles that are very technical, some roles that are very analytical, and some roles that are more traditional: sales, marketing, relationship management, operations, and client services. But ultimately, we're really looking for people who can work together effectively," Marc shared. "You could hire someone who's a rock star with a lot of good ideas but they're not great at working with other people. We would much rather hire someone who's a good team player and knows how to collaborate effectively with other people, and how to interact with clients, than someone who's a rock star but doesn't necessarily work well with others. We're looking for team players more than anything. These are the people who want to be part of something bigger than themselves and will ultimately be the most successful."

I also wanted to know what Marc understood to be the company's biggest obstacle.

"Change is a constant in the financial services industry. Once we became more established we had to figure out how to reinvent ourselves as the needs of clients and the marketplace changed. The company that was here 18 years ago is not the same company that's here today. The clients are in most cases different. The solutions are different. The needs of the marketplace and the regulatory pressures have increased over time. How do you change and evolve as the environment around you is changing? Through the years, Albridge has been very good at addressing the needs of the market and our clients, and we've been able to reinvent ourselves continually."

I wondered what laws of leadership the company has developed, and how they have impacted the business.

"We successfully transitioned from start-up mode into a company which could endure for the long term," Marc said. "The key is to have the right people at the right time. What I always encourage our managers to do is look ahead and ask what your team will need to look like in two to three years.

How will this company effectively serve the marketplace in three years and who are the people that we need on the Albridge team?"

I wanted to know which books inspired Marc. Were there any in particular he shared with team members? Are there insights he follows from a particular author?

Marc said, "There's a book called *The Five Dysfunctions of a Team* by Patrick Lencioni, which I think is a very good, easy-to-read case study in team dynamics. I usually give that book to newer managers."

Marc was also influenced by *The Breakthrough Imperative: how the best managers get outstanding results* by Mark Gottfredson and Steve Schaubert. "It's about how the best general managers achieve new breakthroughs in the performance of their companies. The data and real-life examples the authors used to get their points across were particularly impressive," he said. "I also enjoyed *Leadership Matters: the CEO survival manual* by Mike Myatt. Mike is one of the most highly regarded executive coaches and brings real-world experiences in having led companies himself. I follow his work closely. Regardless of what business or industry you're in, people would find benefit in reading these books."

The best way for readers to find out more is through LinkedIn and at www.albridge.com. "I'm fairly active on LinkedIn and believe in having a strong network. The other way is through my personal contact information. I'm very open to connecting with new people. LinkedIn usually provides a good platform for doing that, but if somebody wants to call or email me directly, I encourage them to do so," Marc said.

Chad Miller, LockNet

It's about having the right people on the team.

LockNet works with leading chain establishments, property managers, access control integrators and general contractors to make doors and locks one less thing they need to worry about. Established in 1993, they are family owned and operated. They collaborate with companies to develop and deliver custom solutions to their unique set of door, lock and hardware needs.

One of the more interesting things about speaking to all these dynamic CEOs is learning that even among the great diversity in their business offerings, many of them echo similar leadership advice. When I asked Chad what elements had to come together to enable the company to celebrate 25 years in business, he said, "To be successful in business there are so many different components that have to come together and work well together at least in the long term. In the short term, luck or other components can come into play, but long term, it takes a lot of pieces working well together."

Just like Marc from Albridge, Chad went on to say, "I think

one of the foundational components, and it almost feels cliché in the business world today, but it's having the right people on the team and having them in the right seats within the organization. When I think about the foundation of our business, it is our people, and the people knowing what they need to do on a daily basis and how that fits into the vision, and how the work that they're doing contributes towards that vision. Without the right people in the right seats, you can get a few things right but you aren't really going to succeed and excel like you could otherwise."

I wondered if Chad, and his father Benson, who founded LockNet, knew 25 years ago about the importance of a team, or if it was a revelation that he figured out at a certain point during his career.

He said, "At some innate level, I've always felt that having the right people is important, but I think it's been over the last 10-plus years that it's crystallized how important that truly is. I'm the second generation in this business, so when the company was started in 1993, I was still just a kid watching it grow from the outside. Later, I joined and held different operational roles until ultimately assuming full leadership of the company. My perspective has definitely changed and I've gained a lot of wisdom over the years. Learning about the importance of having the right people in the right seats is something that I think I've done over time, and as we've grown substantially in the number of team members here within our company.

I think when you're a small company, it's easy for a business owner or leader to compensate for challenges. Say you have a team member who isn't exactly the right fit or isn't fully aligned. When you're small you can work around that a little more easily. The bigger you get, the more you have to delegate, and the more you have to rely on the people being the right people, and not only knowing, but owning the vision, as well. It further magnifies the importance of having the right people," Chad finished.

Knowing he had gained a lot of wisdom during the last 25 years, I asked Chad if he would elaborate a little bit on any leadership laws he's maybe written down or shared with his employees.

"There are two foundational pieces. Firstly, there are the guiding principles that we have for our company," he said. "A lot of companies refer to them as core values, but we've got a set of six principles that we live by that are ingrained in our culture. We hire and fire by them. Everybody in our company knows and lives them. They're not just something that we hang on the wall and talk about; they're really who we are. So that guides us in leading the right people, and in terms of leadership and culture development, those are key."

I was naturally curious to discover those principles and found them on the website:

1. Safety comes first.
2. I am honest and respectful.
3. I listen and serve others before myself.
4. I am purposeful, constructive, and proactive.
5. I focus on efficiency and continuous improvement.
6. I embrace problems with a positive attitude.

Chad continued, "The third principle speaks loudly to me, and that is, 'I listen and serve others before myself.' I view that as a critical component of leadership: making sure that you understand all your team members, such as what motivates them and what's important to them. I view the golden rule as, 'Do unto others as they would have you do unto them.' That's developing empathy and emotional intelligence. I don't believe that everybody needs to be led and managed the same way, so it's having that ability to adapt to the leadership needs of others and leading them in the way that makes the most sense for them."

Speaking of the wisdom component, Chad said he hears a lot about the importance of spending time working on your business as opposed to working in your business. "I'm a member of several outside peer groups of business owners of different sizes and scales. I've been involved in Vistage for about 10 years. I'm a member of YPO. Then there's another local group that isn't formally organized, but it's made up of local business leaders and owners and we meet monthly. Taking the time to engage with others helps me to understand the challenges and obstacles that others go through. I have the ability to learn from them and also help them solve their problems, as well as help me solve my problems. Sharing the challenges, struggles, and wins of leadership, and owning and running a business and all that is entailed with that, is incredibly beneficial. Taking that time to get out of the business, to interact with others who are working at that same level and same perspective is key to success."

Since the company lists the principles on their website for everybody to see, I can tell they are proud of them. I asked Chad if it took a while to develop those principles, as well as how they were created.

He said, "We've had them formalized for at least 10 years now. The approach that we took wasn't to ask, 'What do we aspire to be and what do we want to be?' Our approach was to question ourselves as owners of the company: personally, who are we? Then, in terms of the culture of the organization and where we are, what reflects reality? To find the commonalities and the overlap and boil that down, so it was a process where we went off-site. It took about two days of doing nothing but this, and evaluating who we are, what our identity is, what's important to us to develop what we called our guiding principles."

LockNet uses the entrepreneurial operating system,

Traction, developed by Gino Wickman. "There's a great section on how to go through that process I just described and identify what your organizational core values are. It's been so long now, I don't remember if we followed that exact format, but I really like Gino Wickman's approach."

It's almost never smooth sailing, particularly over the course of 25 years. What were the big obstacles that LockNet had to overcome to get to where they are, and how did they overcome them?

"There've been so many obstacles and challenges. Some are small and we could get through them in a day, and others, as an organization, really set us back," Chad confessed. "We developed the ability to adapt to change. Things are continually changing within our business, with our employees and their lives, within the markets that we serve, the competitive landscape, and what the competitors are doing. We learned to maintain the mindset of how not only to deal with the change, but embrace the change and be proactive about it; to get to where we, ourselves, are the change agent, the change driver within the industry.

We're far from being perfect at that, but the more we can embrace that that mindset of change is just a part of life and bake that into how we do business, the more prepared we will be to deal with obstacles in the future. Looking back to where we stumbled along the way, we weren't then fully embracing that mindset and attitude. The challenges that we did overcome were when we had that mindset that we were going to get through it. I don't think I can boil it down to one thing, but the ability to adapt and deal with continual change is the essence of my response."

I know that with aspiring entrepreneurs, obstacles are usually thrown their way. I wondered if Chad had an inspirational story about how they handled a situation to get to where they are now.

He said, "One thing that comes to mind is when we hit a stagnant sales growth period around the time of 2008 to 2011. For a couple of years, we were flat, or growing at a slow rate. The world, the economy, a lot had changed during that period, and throughout that time our approach to sales and marketing was to do things the way we had always done them. During our quarterly company meetings, I preached that what got us to where we were wasn't going to get us to where we were going. Over the course of about a year and a half, we did a complete overhaul of both our sales and marketing approaches. We changed our people, processes and branding. We had 100 percent turnover on our outside sales force. We kept the company name and the logo, but we did a complete overhaul of everything else. That set us up for going from years of stagnant growth and some inflationary growth to explosive growth where we've been able to triple the size of the business in the last five years. Having the confidence to make very big changes when we were changing our branding and completely overhauling our sales department was a big, scary change, but we took it on and it's paid dividends for us."

Chad mentioned that he meets with groups of entrepreneurs. I wanted to know which groups he is involved with and how they have helped him grow his business.

"I've been a member of Vistage for 10 years, and it has been a phenomenal experience for me, with the opportunity to learn and take from others, and now over the last five-plus years to be able to give back as well. It's an international organization, but it's made up of local groups. There's a chair who leads a maximum group size of around 17-20 members. We meet once a month. Speakers come in about six or seven months out of the year to speak on topics ranging from leadership to sales to finance to human resources, pretty much anything that relates to business, or your personal life as a business leader, how to keep yourself healthy, how to eat right and how to approach life. Participating in that organization for almost 10 years, sitting down once a month with other business leaders and owners who are facing similar challenges, and having the opportunity to process issues with them has been invaluable to me. More recently, I've joined the Young Presidents Organization, and participation there has been invaluable to me as well.

I wondered how meeting with other CEOs from different businesses gives Chad a wider perspective.

"It's so easy to get caught up in our businesses, in our business specifics, in our industry specifics, and feel like we're special and we're unique. Spending time with other business owners helps us realize that we all have the same set of challenges. They're just masked in different industries and different markets. Finding ways to work together to come up with creative solutions is an invaluable experience."

I was curious to learn any examples of how bringing a struggle to a meeting of fellow business owners and leaders helped Chad shift his perspective and find a solution.

"I'll give you an example of what I think almost every business owner has grappled with. You've got somebody on your team who's a great person. They're doing an okay job, but they're not knocking it out of the park and they're not perfect. You've had the coaching conversations with them and you're not getting anywhere. You like this person, and you have this tendency to keep your head in the sand and just deal with it. Bringing that problem to the group forces the accountability to have those discussions. They ask what's going on in the business; what's keeping you up at night. Those conversations inevitably come out, and it's there where I think that you can have the conversations, be it about an underperforming team member, a customer who isn't the right fit, or some other aspect of your business. You realize other people are dealing with the same challenges, and you get the courage, the confidence, and the support to make a change that doesn't feel comfortable. And then you've got a group of people holding you accountable to it.

There are certain areas that I still consider myself to be very weak in when it comes to business. When we've worked with financing before, it's always been more at a traditional bank level, so I've had introductions to things like mezzanine financing and other private equity firms. There's a whole lot of networking and introductions that can come from those that can be very beneficial to the business. When we started exploring setting up a board of advisors for our company, and outside independent members, I was able to get a lot of very good input from outside peer groups there, and introductions to members who have led to phenomenal additions in setting up an advisory board for our company. Those are things that you just can't get if you're just spending time within your organization.

Finally, there's the adage, 'It's lonely at the top.' As a chief executive officer or president of a company, especially when you're privately held, you might be the majority owner and you make the decisions that will impact all of your employees. Some of the tough calls you can't talk to your employees about, yet you have to make a decision. Having an outside, confidential, trusted peer group where you can talk about those ideas is invaluable for that," Chad said.

Chad must have read a bunch of books. I wondered which ones shaped him as a leader and influenced the way he runs the business.

"There are so many," he said. "It's hard to boil it down to just one or a few. *Good to Great* by Jim Collins goes back to having the right people in the right seats. There's a lot in that book that is fundamental to business, and it's key. About two years ago, I read the Elon Musk biography by Ashlee Vance, and I was blown away by the book. To be completely honest, I've got a complete total man-and-leader crush on Elon. I haven't seen anybody who has the level of vision that he has, and then the ability to execute on that, and not just execute it on the high level, but down to engineering the rockets for SpaceX, staying up all night writing the code to make things happen, and his ability to inspire others and get them to follow along with his vision. I'm sure he's by no means perfect and free of some of the perils that all business owners face, but his ability to paint a vision such as, 'I don't want to run a successful business but I want to make it so that humanity can survive by colonizing Mars,' and then getting people to rally around that, getting a business built around it, just blows me away. So that's been incredibly inspirational to me," Chad said.

"I like to read a lot of books that touch on peripherals of leadership. There's *Extreme Ownership* by Jocko Willink and his need to see how a lot of ideas and concepts were brought in from the military and special forces units and how that applies to leadership. The Steve Jobs biography — I think he was a real jerk in many respects, but he was able to build incredibly successful companies, and again, the amount of vision that he had and his ability to inspire others was amazing. He and his way doesn't fit within the guiding principles of LockNet, but I still think there's a whole lot to be learned from Steve Jobs and what he did. I'm big on biographies.

A few other books that have been inspirational to me and I think are must reads for any business owner/leader are:

The Everything Store by Jeff Bezos
Delivering Happiness by Tony Hsieh
The Virgin Way by Richard Branson
Traction by Gino Wickman
The E-Myth Revisited by Michael Gerber

To learn more about Chad and LockNet you can visit www.locknet.com.

Steve Olsher, Liquor.com

Forgive and forget.

Liquor.com is the inspiring digital publication dedicated to good drinking and great living: the right cocktail at the right time; home-entertaining advice; essential recipes and indispensable spirits; the people and places that matter now. Liquor.com and its stories have won numerous awards, including for Best Cocktail Writing and Best Cocktail Author at the 2012 Tales of the Cocktail Spirited Awards, and a James Beard Award in 2013 for its *How to Cocktail* video series.

Their site has a huge network of award-winning writers, master mixologists and spirits experts who travel the globe to find the perfect drink, as well as a top-shelf board of advisors. Liquor.com considers itself the experienced drinking buddy, who not only knows what to drink and where, but also when to stir and when to shake, when to shoot and when to sip, and when to splurge and when to save. Their goal is to entertain, inspire and educate enthusiasts, connoisseurs and even the merely curious about the vast universe of cocktails and spirits. The site combines old-school editorial experience with the newest web technologies.

Chairman Steve Olsher said when he started Liquor.com in 1993, he first needed to understand where the future of communication was going. "Back then it was CompuServe, and America Online, and Earthlink. The medium itself does all the heavy lifting in terms of attracting people to the platform. All we have to do is give folks something to do on that platform.

Whether it's being entertained, or connecting, or shopping, or discussing those sorts of things, that is what folks look to do in a communal environment online. It becomes a question of what you're going to do on that platform. One of the reasons why I've been able to do as well as I've been able to do over the years online is because people are always going to be looking for something to do on that medium. At the end of the day, it's my job and my responsibility to provide one of those means of engagement," Steve explained. "It boils down to finding the right means of engagement, and tapping into those who don't know what else to do on that medium."

I wanted to know about Steve's early vision when he started the company in 1993. Is he now where he expected he would be?

Steve said, "The vision at the time was 'Let's do whatever we can do to gain more visibility for our company.' We were looking for a means with which to create more visibility, and get more eyeballs on what we were doing as a company. Nothing mind-blowing, nothing mind-boggling, but it simply seemed like that was where a lot of the attention was going, and I knew we had to be at the forefront of it all."

Since Steve's business is an online one, I was curious about the types of obstacles his company faced during their 25 years in business.

"During 25 years online, a lot changes, and you have to adapt. It boils down to staying on top of what's changing in the online space," Steve explained. "You have to think from the standpoint of your readers. If people are reading more, then you have to write longer articles. If people are wanting those articles on video, then you have to create that same content on video. If people can't watch video, and they're shifting towards audio, then you obviously have to provide that content as well. It's all about delivering the content in the manner in which people want to consume it, and that's been the biggest change for us."

I asked Steve about his early motivations when starting his business. He said that as an entrepreneur he is certainly motivated by the ability to profit. "There's no sharking that, and I'm certainly not apologetic for it. I think that when you have something that the people want and it's your goal, your job, and your obligation to make it available to them, and you can profit in the process, then by all means you should. For me, it was about being able to create something that solved a need. It's about understanding what the problems are, and then providing solutions, and when those solutions create new problems you need to create new solutions.

How it all trickled down for me was to do whatever we could to address the problems that people were having in their respective spaces. To get them solved. Ultimately, I believe any entrepreneurial endeavor should be driven by the opportunity to profit," Steve explained. "For example, my family was in the liquor business, so my business was simply the evolution of the business that my grandfather started back in 1939. I took it in a different direction within the same industry."

Certainly, entrepreneurs need to adapt, and Steve needed to adapt in the last 25 years. Since a lot of things changed online, I wondered if there were any particularly big changes to which he had to adapt. Indeed there were.

"We would rely on other platforms to host our stores.

CompuServe was a perfect example. We launched on CompuServe's electronic mall, but then we became very reliant on that platform, and our business lived or died with the stability and attractiveness of that platform. One of the biggest things that we had to do early on was to build our own e-commerce site from scratch," Steve explained. "At the time, there were no Shopifys, and no shopping cart type programs, so we had to kick the creation of our own platform into gear and give ourselves the opportunity to be not so reliant on others.

I think it holds true today — whether it's with podcasting, or blogging, or video marketing, whatever it might be — that having your own platform with which you drive your traffic rather than being dependent on Facebook, or YouTube, or one of those platforms ultimately is where we need to be with our content, and with our offerings," Steve said. "Certainly one of the ways that we need to adapt is by getting things onto our own platforms, and being able to control that process. When people rely on third party platforms, it only goes so far."

I was curious to know since Steve took over or developed the online part of the business his grandfather started, whether there were any laws of leadership already set in stone that Steve continues to follow, or did Steve develop some laws of his own.

"My grandfather was certainly my first mentor. No doubt at all. I learned quite a bit from him, and a couple of things that I learned revolve around relationships," Steve said. "His philosophy was to forgive and forget. There will always be people in business who potentially are going to do things that wouldn't be perceived so well in the real world. My grandfather's philosophy is that you have to move beyond that and forgive those for their trespasses no matter what those are. No matter how you slice it, people are human. To hold on to any of that hurt or pain continues to give them power over you. That's one of the lessons that I learned from him: you've got to move on, and you've got to learn how to forgive.

Look, I certainly have my moments where it's more difficult than others to do so for sure. For the most part I try not to dwell, or hold onto too much. This is definitely something I learned from my grandfather, and incorporate in my daily life. I have my lapses, but for the most part his advice certainly sticks," Steve said.

Another thing Steve learned from his grandfather is to honor his gut feeling. "It's really important to listen to and honor your gut, and to be willing to cut the rope even when you don't yet know if that's the right choice. The odds of it being the right choice if your gut tells you so are pretty good. I believe one of the things most people find very, very difficult to do is to make those tough decisions, and to cut the rope on what might have seemed promising, but ultimately is not bearing fruit in the way that they had envisioned."

Steve feels that leadership boils down to managing the emotions and expectations of your team. "If you recognize that's your job as a leader, then you're going to be able to surround yourself with people who are able to operate in their own zones of genius, and do what they do best, as you allow them to do what they do best. Ultimately, you've got to guide them with how to become the best version of who it is that they were meant and made to be."

Steve is an author, and his book *What is Your WHAT?* is his most popular. I was curious to know which other books have influenced him in the way he conducts business, and influenced what he wrote in *What is Your WHAT*?

Like many leaders, Steve is a big reader. "To go back though the tried and true reads that I've had over the years, the first would be *Guerrilla Marketing* by Jay Conrad Levinson. It's an unbelievably well-written book that was way ahead of its time. Certainly, *Guerrilla Marketing* would be one of those books that I would recommend to anyone. Covey's *The 7 Habits of Highly Effective People* is always going to make that list for me, no doubt about that. Jack Canfield's *The Success Principles* is certainly one of them as well. For more of a modern flair, Russell Brunson has a very good book called *DotCom Secrets*, as well as *Expert Secrets*. Both books are very good in terms of laying out what to do, and how to do it in this online world. It's amazing actually how much he shares with his readers."

I asked Steve to tell me a little more about his book, *What Is Your WHAT?*, particularly in terms of what readers can expect to learn from it.

Steve said *What Is Your WHAT?* is all about how to discover that one amazing thing you were truly born to do. "I believe that we are each naturally wired to excel in very specific ways. This book is about how to discover your core gift, and how to discover the primary vehicle you use to share that gift, and then how to identify the people that you're most compelled to serve. It's the combination of the gifts, the vehicle and the people that make up the *What is Your WHAT?* framework. It's definitely helpful for those who are trying to figure out how to get started in business, and exactly what to do. This book is about how to bring that to the surface so you can really pursue that with strategic abandon."

Steve said, "The best way to learn more is certainly to start with the book, and you can grab a free copy at whatisyourwhat.com. Reinvention Radio would be the next best thing to explore. Ultimately, we cover a lot of ground, and you'll figure out pretty quickly if you like what I'm up to." To learn more about Steve and Liquor.com, you can visit www.liquor.com.

Ali Razi, Banc Certified Merchant Services

Take care of your staff.

Formed over two decades ago, Banc Certified Merchant Services (BCMS) is a worldwide full-service Merchant Services Provider offering a wide variety of products and services to merchants. BCMS is a leader in the merchant services industry; they enjoy the distinction of being the processor of choice for many respected merchants in the world. They have grown to handle more than $350 million a month in processing transactions while maintaining an A+ rating with the Better Business Bureau. The ongoing success of BCMS is the result of focusing on superior customer service. BCMS believes that every merchant deserves the best.

It's easy to see many commonalities amongst our CEOs as we head toward the end of our interviews. The statistics claim that eight out of ten entrepreneurs fail within the first 18 months of starting their business and then only one-third of businesses will actually make it past their tenth year. I ask Ali what he thinks is the No.1 factor to which he attitudes his success with Banc Certified.

"To put it simply, success comes from taking care of my staff and taking care of my clients, in that order, because if you take care of your staff, they'll take care of your clients," he explained. "In our company, we are very liberal with our time off. We provide our employees with loans and advances. We provide them with opportunities to move very rapidly. We are a very employee-aware company because we realize they are our No.1 asset. I talk to a lot of fellow business owners, and they agree that the biggest asset the company has is its employees. Their worth is not measured anywhere in the financial statements, which is unfortunate, as tables, doors and chairs don't sell or pick up clients."

What a quote!

Ali continued, "It's rather unfortunate that in today's world loyalty is diminishing on both fronts. Many of the younger generation seem to think they can only move by changing jobs every eight months. Short term, it works, but in the long term that path has very big problems. It's the same with companies: employees are just a number. GE just announced they're going to lay off 12,000 people right before Christmas.

Where is the heart? What kind of loyalty are you going to expect in return from the remaining force when you let 12,000 people know right before the holidays you're going to let them go? Why couldn't they wait until after the holidays?" Ali asked. "The problem is in this country unfortunately everybody is managed on a very short time frame — which is three months — and we report to the stock market, and that's what drives every valuation. You look at some companies like Facebook. How can Facebook be more valuable than GE? Facebook doesn't own anything. It's just an idea that can be owned just like other businesses that have come before, such as MySpace, which is now gone. The same thing is going to happen to Facebook, except they're a lot surer than most businesses.

When a CEO announces 12,000 people are going to go right before the holidays, he is obviously doing it for the fourth-quarter reaction to the market, without even thinking about what's going to happen to these 12,000 families. When you figure each family has three members, that's 36,000 people that he just affected right before Christmas," Ali said.

"CEOs don't provide loyalty to their employees, and employees don't have any loyalty in return. That's a big problem. Smaller companies like us, who are private, don't have to report to anyone except the IRS at the end of the year. I can make all kinds of decisions throughout the year, which in a quarter-by-quarter sense may not be a smart move, but over the long term it's a great move.

For example, we give loans to our staff, and provide them with help. Our employees get involved in charities, as we each choose our own charitable organizations for charitable giving. We ask our staff which charity they're involved in and that's what we get involved in to encourage them. If they do it, we're right behind them," Ali said.

It's fantastic how much Ali invests in his employees. I asked him how he helps his employees to feel invested in the company.

"When you look at the annual bonuses given to employees, usually somebody sits behind the mahogany desk and looks at some metrics and decides, 'Okay, here's a bonus these people get.' For our year-end bonus, we distribute 10 percent of our income to our staff," Ali said. "The staff members vote on who gets what, so it creates a tremendous amount of camaraderie among them when they decide and they vote. Whoever gets the most votes based on the total number of votes, that's the person, that's just the pool they get. All through the year, the employees know if they help their fellow worker, at the end of the year, when it comes to the voting for the bonuses, they're going to vote for them and they get a bigger chunk. This is as opposed to me sitting behind my desk and deciding who gets what.

I asked Ali about overcoming obstacles he has encountered during his 25 years in business, and he echoed some thoughts common to several of our other CEOs.

The biggest obstacle for Ali was to manage the company's growth. "If you grow too fast, you're going to cause negative and catastrophic consequences. If you grow too slowly, you're going to go out of business. So in managing that growth, you must make sure that, like our company, you are almost debt free. You don't have any debt to any organization, and you're not backed by some guy on Wall Street who runs a venture firm or a private equity firm because those guys destroy businesses.

All of our growth has been organic. We funded our own growth, so it has been our ability to manage growth to make sure our finances keep up with it, and to make sure we make investments in the right areas. If we do make mistakes and we miscalculate, we correct it and move away from it quickly," Ali said.

When talking about business growth, I wondered if Ali was referring to growing numbers of clients.

"Our infrastructure can handle hundreds of clients, but I must ensure that we have the overhead to support that clientele. We provide electronic payment processing, so we can double our client base without much of an issue. It's more of a matter of making sure we have the trained account executives, and we have the trained support people, and the trained sales people to take care of this clientele," Ali explained. "That's why we have such a great reputation. We're A+ at the Better Business Bureau, for example. That credit goes to my staff, in the way they take care of our clientele.

The challenge is to make sure that first and foremost you're able to recruit the right people. Unemployment is very low now, so finding the right people at times can be difficult, especially if you're at a giant company or a small business and you want to attract employees. Our total head count is about 300 people. We have to make sure we find the right people. For example, we have to know what makes somebody want to work for a company our size, as opposed to working for GE. We have to make sure we can manage our growth with the right personnel," Ali said.

It turned out that Ali had some very simple, tried-and-true guiding principles or laws of leadership.

"Lead by example, No.1. And No.2, if it was easy, everybody would do it," he said. "I am not going to go to my staff and ask them to do something that I wouldn't be willing to do. At our company we have a very strict work day. We work 9-5. Our doors are shut by 5.05. We don't want our staff to work here until 8 o'clock at night. If you work 9-5 — and you really work — you're going to get the day's work done. When five o'clock arrives, I want them to go home and be with their family. We are very aware of our staff's family life. We don't work on the weekends, as that is the time you spend with your family. But 9-5, when you are at the office, let's work and let's take care of our clients."

Since Banc Certified does payment processing, and Ali is dedicated to his employees having their time off, I asked how the after-hours and outside-hours help is handled.

"Our customer support is 24 hours a day, 365 days a year, but our customer support is provided by our payment processors. They provide the 24-hour support. We have our own support but that's only 9-5; after that, all the support goes to the payment-processing companies that we work with. We mostly deal with businesses. We have very few retail operations, so we mostly deal with businesses who are open 9-5," Ali explained.

I asked Ali to elaborate on his second guiding principle, 'If it was easy, everybody would be doing it'.

"Because I'm a very hard-working guy, I make sure that our staff understands the reason that we are in business. It's not easy to remain in business. Statistics say that right at the beginning, the odds are against you. Not only do we have competition from inside our country, we have tremendous competition from foreign entities. We are in a very competitive world. At times, things are not easy, which is a good thing, because if it was easy, everybody would be a businessman," Ali said.

"I'm an entrepreneur and I make sure every employee that we have has an entrepreneur mentality. We need to be better. We compete with Chase, Wells Fargo, U.S. Bank and other major banks. How are we going to compete with these guys if we don't have something special to offer?

The example I always give is if you need heart surgery, you can go to a heart surgeon or you can go to a general surgeon. Which one would you go to? Obviously, you want to go to the specialist, the heart surgeon. That's what we are, that's all we do, so we have to be the best at it. We have to be constantly innovative," Ali said. "We have developed some of our own technology. Some of the stuff that we have, no competition of ours has, and that's the advantage of being a privately-held company because I don't have a board of directors that has to approve every move I make," Ali said.

I was curious to know which books most motivated Ali and influenced the way he runs his business.

"The first one that has made a tremendous impact on my business and on me is *Who Moved My Cheese?* by Spencer Johnson. The second one is *Good to Great* by Jim Collins. And the third one is *Mad Genius* by Randy Gage. Obviously, there are so many great books, but these are the three that from all the business books that I've read, have made the most impact on my daily running of a business," Ali said.

"For example, in *Who Moved My Cheese?*, I learned the importance of not getting so set in your ways that you cannot change and adapt. If you look at the Fortune 500 companies of 60 years ago, I think 10 of them are still in business. They get so set in their own ways that they can't adjust.

The next one is *Good to Great*, which talks about how as a businessman you operate a bus. I'm a bus driver and I have so many seats. How do I take this company from being good to being great? Who do I choose to fill the seats? Those are my employees," Ali said. "*Mad Genius* talks about the different ways of running your business, marketing strategies and things like that. It talks about us entrepreneurs being like an artist. We create art. Just like with an artist, we start with a white canvas, and after so many hours, it's a beautiful artwork. Your business should be a work of art."

Ali would like to write a book combining his life stories and role in business. He said something I think many of our entrepreneurs can relate to.

"Like any other businessman, my first businesses failed — five of them in my case. What makes an entrepreneur keep going? You'd think that after having five failed businesses, your sixth one is going to be successful. That's what an entrepreneur is: a person who just keeps going. I've never received a paycheck that doesn't have my signature on it. I've never worked for anyone else. I'm an entrepreneur."

To learn more about Ali and Banc Certified Merchant Services, you can visit www.banccertified.com.

David Fuess, Catapult Systems

Hiring wisely is the No.1 factor.

On the landing page of Catapult Systems, visitors read, "We imagine, build and sustain IT-enabled business solutions that people love to use. Catapult Systems is a modern digital solutions and services firm that specializes in emerging and business-critical technologies." One immediately gets the impression that the company is all about people.

I asked CEO David Fuess what he considers to be the reasons for their quarter century of success.

He believes that hiring wisely is the No.1 factor. "There are so many factors that go into a successful business, but if one rises above the other, it would be that. The business that I'm in is consulting, and so it's a people-intensive business. We recognized early on that in the hires that we were going to be making, employees are our biggest asset. You've probably heard that before. It's a bit of a cliché, but it's absolutely true.

We implemented a hiring and interview methodology called top grading, which was invented by General Electric a couple of dozen years ago. It proved to be probably one of the smartest things we have ever done. Our ability to interview people to determine if they're what we call 'A players' has been extremely successful for us. Occasionally, we make a bad decision or a bad hire, but it's pretty rare that someone gets through our seven-step process and they're not an A player," David said.

"People are at the top, and hiring them is the first half of the equation. The second half is keeping them. We have instituted many programs that are all designed to make it a great place to work. We've been awarded best place to work in Texas and in the various cities that we're in so many times that I can't even keep up. It's probably 50 times over 25 years.

So we get talented people with great attitudes, and then we keep them for a long time. My executive team — my direct reports, which is about 10 people — have been with the company more than 10 years and some of them have been with the company over 20 years," David said.

Naturally, I was curious to know about Catapult's seven-step process and the criteria that they look for to make wise hires.

"If any readers want to do more investigation, you can find plenty of information out there. The process is called top grading. The whole idea behind it is to find A players, and there is a definition behind them. It does not mean someone with the most experience. Even if you're hiring someone who is working at the reception desk, you're looking for an A player to do that job. That's a different set of qualifications than if you're looking for a chief financial officer or a software architect," David explained.

"We start with a very good definition of the role, and then we go through a culture interview early on to determine if this person is someone that we would all want to be with 50 to 60 hours a week, whatever's required. We take them back all the way to junior high in what's called a CIDS interview, a chronological in-depth interview. That's actually the last stage of the seven-step process, but it's to make sure that we thoroughly understand this person as a person."

David explained that this is not a technical interview. "It's a 'Walk me through your life and what your high-school teacher would have said about you' kind of interview. It's a refined method of finding out if they have the right technical skills, people skills, communication skills and the right constitution as a human being to work with us. By the time they get to that seventh step, they're a little tired. That's right when you get the best information, so it's very intentional, as well.

I would say the people that join the company greatly appreciate that process. They're going to invest a lot of time in us, and most companies do one or two interviews and make a hire/no hire decision. I think that leaves the candidate feeling a little slighted sometimes, even though they got the job. Ours is just the opposite. People feel like we care, and it's because we do," David said. "We try to move it through pretty quickly. Usually within a couple of weeks, we can get it done. It's actually seven different people who interview the person, with me many times, depending on the role, but many times, I'm doing the final interview."

I wanted to know more about some of the programs Catapult employs to keep top talent engaged and happy.

"We have core values like most companies do, but the way we recognize people for core value awards — which we do monthly at our company meetings — is by letting people's colleagues nominate them for core-value awards including teamwork, initiative, passion and a few others. The people celebrate each other and highlight it at each company meeting. Speaking of company meetings, we have an in-person, once a month, in-each-office company meeting, and we keep it kind of casual. It's casual and it's a PowerPoint, and we let people bring a beer or a glass of wine and then we bring some food in," David said.

That communication is very important. "We are 100 percent open-book financials, good, bad, or ugly. Our employees very much appreciate that. We have quarterly events with our employees in each of our markets. It could be that everybody goes bowling or everyone goes to a pool hall. It is decided by the people what to do with our quarterly events.

We also look for opportunities to get spouses and significant others involved, because I think it's important for them to see what their significant other is working with. The company's getting fairly large and so it's getting harder, but I like to get to know their families and their husband or wife or significant other and their kids' names," David said.

"Speaking of kids, we do an annual themed kids event in July of each year, and each of the kids under 13 is invited. It's a huge highlight. This one was 'Under the Sea', so it was doing lots of games and teaching the kids about things in the ocean, which they thoroughly enjoyed. We've been doing this for 12 years, and we get feedback that it's the highlight of the year. Most of the time, if you get the employees' kids connected into the company, it's a retention tool," David explained.

"Good people get offered jobs all the time, and so we have to do things to keep them engaged. I also do a bronze club with every person that has been with the company one year, and we also have a gold, a platinum and a diamond club at three, five and 10 years. We have an annual holiday party in every one of our offices that spouses are invited to and it's always a good time.

We have an idea inbox, where anyone in the company at any time can make any suggestion about things we could be doing better, or things that we are doing well and they want us to keep doing. Probably one of the most unique programs we have is called the Dream Machine. The Dream Machine is where the company has put a nest egg aside to support people or their immediate families in the company that have needs," David said.

"I'll give you an example. We had an employee's mother who lived in Florida and the employee lived in San Antonio. One of her colleagues said, 'Hey, so and so is unable to get to Florida. She doesn't have enough vacation left and it's expensive last minute to go see her mom, but she would really like to do that.' This communication comes to the executive team immediately when someone makes a Dream Machine request, and so the next day we approved it and we gave her three days of vacation and we paid for her ticket to go see her mom," David said. "That's just one of 100 stories I could tell, but it's those sorts of things we do that really matter. We don't run it like it's all about money. It's all about people, yet we need to make money in the process."

Wow! David's employees must really feel appreciated. I asked him to tell me more about the bronze and different level clubs at Catapult.

"The bronze club is a CEO lunch. They're always shocked, which always shocks me, that a CEO would take time to visit someone who's been with us a year. It's usually five to ten people at a time, and we thank them for being with us. We know that there are a lot of other places who are wanting their time and services, and want them to come work for them," David explained. "So we thank them for being with us, and ask what it is that keeps bringing them back to work at Catapult each day. That's a learning thing for us to ensure that we continue to do the things that have attracted the great talent we have.

I also open it up to the bad and the ugly. That might be saying to the employee, 'You've been here a year now. The honeymoon has worn off. You probably have seen some things that you feel like we could do better. We're not perfect. We're always trying to improve.' The benefit is a direct relationship with me and being able to share openly and have no repercussions. No one will ever get in any sort of trouble based on what they tell me in a bronze-club meeting. It's anonymous from that perspective," David said. "For the gold and the platinum and the diamond, we give them gift certificates of different amounts for each year that they're with us. I believe one of them was $500, and then the diamond club is $1,000, and it's an Amazon gift card and a personally written note from me thanking them for their tenure."

It was no surprise to learn that one of the biggest obstacles Catapult had to overcome was the dot-com bust. David said, "We're in high tech, and we're headquartered in Austin, Texas, so that was the most challenging thing that we've ever been through. At that time, in 2001, about 30 percent of our revenue came from dot-coms. In a period of less than 60 days, every single bit of those customers folded. Not only did we lose 30 percent of our revenue, but all of a sudden, we had no profits to go along with that, and those companies were never going to pay their bills. It was a triple-combination thing."

Surviving this shock necessitated that Catapult take a combination of actions. "We looked at every single job carefully. We were sure to treat the situation with as much humanity as possible, and I personally visited with every single person we did have to let go. The smartest thing we did was ask every single person in the company we were able to retain — which was about 60 percent — to take a 10 percent pay cut, including me. Everybody knew that they were going to participate together as a team and give our all back to the right place. They knew that what happened wasn't our fault, but we still had to make decisions about how to respond to it in a way that kept the energy and the spirit of the company alive," David said. "What's interesting is a couple of years later, by the time things were back to normal, quite a number of those folks we had to let go came back to work for us. It wasn't just one or two. It was a dozen or more."

I asked David about the specific laws of leadership he has developed in his 25-year career.

"Probably like most of the CEOs you've talked to, I've read all the books. I've gleaned things here and there, and then made it my own. I could get theoretical with you, or maybe textbook, but I'll tell you for me it boils down to three things that permeate our organization.

The first one is to be humble. We have a lot of highly educated people. We're in an industry where our consultants are getting a lot of complimentary feedback from our customers, and it's very easy to start taking yourself too seriously and get what I call 'the wide-receiver syndrome,' where it's all about me, as in, 'Give me the ball and I'm going to score a touchdown.' We try to be the opposite of that here. We stay humble," David said.

The second thing David espouses is to be kind to one another. "I know that sounds basic, but people aren't kind enough to each other out there in the world. It's so important to be kind. If you know everybody on your team has your back and you've got their back, it changes the complete dynamic of teamwork. We are in very much a team sport. These consultants are working together to go accomplish software-related tasks.

The last one is when necessary, be tough as nails. What I mean by that is when you're humble and when you're kind to each other, sometimes people want to take advantage of you. They think you're soft or maybe willing to be taken advantage of. We are not by being humble and kind to one another going to be taken advantage of. When that happens — and unfortunately, it's usually a client that's trying to take advantage of us — it's important to be able to stand your ground. You have to know when that situation calls for it and when it does, you've got to be as tough as nails," David finished.

David mentioned that he's read all the books, so I asked him to tell me which book has influenced him the most and the way he conducts business.

"As background before answering that question, over the last three years we have been transforming our business. It's been a requirement as the cloud has come about to reinvent ourselves and sell new services in a different way. Without getting into too much detail there because I don't think it's required, I read a book called *Freakonomics* by Stephen J. Dubner and Steven Levitt. It really changed the way I thought about things going into this transformation.

We were entering a period where we were going to have to take some risks. There was no way to see around some of the corners that we were going to have to be able to get around. Sometimes you have to put more than one line in the water, so to speak. You have to take three or four calculated risks knowing that maybe one of them will pan out. It'd be great if all three or four did, but that's not the way it usually works. We had to make investments of people, time, money — all of our resources — to put into these various strategies.

What I learned from *Freakonomics* is that the best thing that we could do is fail fast. Don't be afraid to fail, but know what failure is, have it defined, and when you hit that fork in the road, call it what it is and actually celebrate it, which is completely opposite of what people would expect. People are afraid of making mistakes, and they certainly never celebrate a failure. We're going to learn from it, and we're going to fail fast. Every step along the way, we ask ourselves if we are going in the right direction. It ties into being humble. We could get very proud in our ideas sometimes. Instead, let's learn how to fail fast. We've done it. We have failed a few times. We've also hit it out of the park a few times. That book had probably more impact on me at just the right time than any one in the last four years or so," David said.

To learn more about David and Catapult Systems, you can visit www.catapultsystems.com and check out the leadership team. David said, "For good, bad, or ugly, if you Google my name and Catapult, you see a fair amount of press releases, so you certainly could do it that way, too."

Your Team

Now you know what the six ingredients of supreme leadership are. You need passion, vision, persistence, adaptability, customer centeredness and relationships.

But what if you're underperforming in one or two of them? While you can't "learn" passion, you can find something that you're passionate about and build your business around it. The other five ingredients are all, to some extent, "learnable" skills.

A common concern numerous leaders I interviewed raised was how they keep a strong leadership once they are no longer active in their roles.

One way is to grow the next generation of leaders internally. All the CEOs I interviewed shared books that impacted the way they conduct business. Many buy additional copies for their team members so that they can grow as well and understand the motivation that drives their leader.

If you want your team members to share your passion, your vision, your persistence, your ability to adapt, your focus on customers and your skill at building thriving relationships, make sure to drop a copy of *Supreme Leadership* on their desks.

Acknowledgements

To Dean Jackson, the marketing buddha, who helped me soar to new heights by coming up with the idea for this book.

To my brother, Tomasz Rutkowski, CEO of Senfino, who suggested a fool-proof way of connecting with leaders featured on the pages of this publication.

To my friends at RightHello, who did all the heavy lifting of emailing hundreds of companies to be able to feature the selected few.

To Evelyn Jackson and Deborah Brannon, who helped me interview featured leaders, picking their minds for their secrets to success.

To Marlayna Glynn, who took the interview transcripts I threw at her and turned them into this spectacular material.

To Andrew Whiteside, my long-time friend and trusted copy-editor, who diligently checks every writing piece I produce.

About the Author

Alinka Rutkowska has always been fascinated by leaders and leadership. In fact, her dissertation in business school was on leadership.

After graduating from Warsaw School of Economics and achieving a CEMS master's degree from Luigi Bocconi University in Milan, she went on to climb the corporate ladder in multinational companies.

She published her first book back in 2010 and got the CEO's blessing to pursue a career in publishing.

She's now a multi-award-winning and #1 international bestselling author. She's a coach who transforms struggling writers into profitable authorpreneurs via her Author Remake platform.

Her acclaimed title *How I Sold 80,000 Books* is a must-read for every new author.

Since her full immersion in publishing, she has founded LibraryBub, the first service to connect librarians with award-winning and bestselling books from independent publishers.

She has created and hosted the 5-Figure Author Challenge, which gives authors winning strategies to get to 5 figures in 5 months.

She's been featured on Fox Business Network, affiliates of ABC, NBC and CBS, Author Marketing Club, The Author

Hangout, Kindlepreneur, Book Marketing Mentors, Examiner, She Knows, She Writes, The Writer's Life and many more.

She's a sought-after speaker and has spoken at numerous conferences and on podcasts. She was voted a Top 5 speaker and named most creative book marketer at the Bestseller Summit Online.

Alinka is now passionate about helping leaders to create their own books, which increase their authority, visibility and allow them to add to their legacy of learning.